W9-AXB-606

A SEASON OF LOSS
A LIFETIME OF FORGIVENESS

A SEASON OF LOSS
A LIFETIME OF FORGIVENESS

THE DAN SNYDER
AND DANY HEATLEY STORY

JOHN MANASSO

ECW PRESS

Copyright © John Manasso, 2005

Published by ECW Press
2120 Queen Street East, Suite 200, Toronto, Ontario, Canada M4E 1E2

All rights reserved. No part of this publication may be reproduced, stored
in a retrieval system, or transmitted in any form by any process — electronic,
mechanical, photocopying, recording, or otherwise — without the prior
written permission of the copyright owners and ECW Press.

LIBRARY AND ARCHIVES CANADA CATALOGUING IN PUBLICATION

Manasso, John
A season of loss, a lifetime of foregiveness : the Dan Snyder and Dany
Heatley story / John Manasso.

ISBN 1-55022-702-5

1. Snyder, Dan, 1978–2003—Death and burial. 2. Heatley, Dany. 3. Hockey players—
Canada—Biography. 4. Traffic accident victims —
Biography. I. Title.

GV848.5.A1M35 2005   796.962'092271   C2005-904375-X

Copy editor: Kevin Connolly
Cover and Text Design: Tania Craan
Production: Mary Bowness
Cover Photo: Courtesy of the Atlanta Thrashers
Printing: Friesens

This book is set in Minion and Trajan

Heaven Is a Better Place Today, written by: Baker, Downie, Fay, Langlois, Sinclair
Used by Permission of Little Smoke / peermusic Canada, Inc.

5 4 3 2

DISTRIBUTION

CANADA: Jaguar Book Group, 100 Armstrong Ave., Georgetown, ON L7G 5S4
UNITED STATES: Independent Publishers Group, 814 North Franklin Street,
Chicago, IL, U.S.A. 60610

PRINTED AND BOUND IN CANADA

ECW PRESS
ecwpress.com

To Joey and Sam

ACKNOWLEDGEMENTS

This book would not have been possible without the cooperation of Graham, LuAnn, Jake and Erika Snyder. I would like to thank them for allowing me into their home, into their most intimate memories and for the many hours spent on the phone, which were at times tearful, at times difficult and at others filled with laughter. Some of the materials they supplied — Graham sifted through Erika's countless videos of the *Gilmore Girls* to find tapes that related to Dan from before and after his death — were invaluable. The significance those tapes held was not lost on me as I brought them to Atlanta from Elmira and it was no small weight lifted from my shoulders when I had safely placed them back in Graham's hands. Another invaluable contribution to this book came in sorting through the thousands of letters of support and condolence the Snyders received — words which, in themselves could fill their own book. These letters once again caused them to relive difficult times. I would also like to thank them for giving their blessing to those who were unsure whether to talk to me when I first came calling. The names, phone numbers, addresses and e-mail addresses they supplied were invaluable.

I would like to thank ECW Press publisher Jack David for sharing the same vision as I had for this book, which was one more about a family's journey through grief and forgiveness than it was one about the sport of hockey. My editor Michael Holmes' critiques made for greater accuracy and better writing. I also want to thank the rest of the staff at ECW for their role in getting this to press and the work they did to improve the overall product and its salability. And special thanks to Greg Dinkin, who put me in touch with ECW, and made this project possible.

I also would like to thank my editors at the *Journal–Constitution* for giving me permission to pursue this side project, especially Don Boykin and Ronnie Ramos. Particular thanks goes to Chris Vivlamore, who, during the NHL lockout, acceded to my requests to cover events in Detroit and Toronto that made it possible to stay a few extra days in Elmira so I could do research and conduct interviews. I also would like to thank *Journal–Constitution* columnist Jeff Schultz, who somehow covered the Thrashers beat through the misery of the team's first three expansion seasons and whose sensitivity and insight in writing about Dany Heatley's car accident, and later Dan Snyder's funeral, paved the way for my future articles and, ultimately, this book.

I would like to thank everyone who was interviewed, or who helped to put me in touch with someone for an interview, for either my newspaper articles, some of which were included in the book, or the book itself: Ruth Anne Laverty, Larry Devitt, Linda Bell, Gerlinde Petz, Dean Peachey, Mark Yantzi, Joseph Snyder, Deb Good, William Cassino, Dan Marr, Don Waddell, Bob Hartley, Rob Koch, Tom Hughes, the Thrashers organization, Bruce Levenson, Rutherford Seydel, Mark Johnson, Ryan Christie, Joey Guilmet, Garnet Exelby, J.P. Vigier, Ben Simon, Slava Kozlov, Brad Tapper, Jarrod Skalde, Kevin Cheveldayoff, Tom Langley, Don Samuel, Manny Arora, Mark Tate, the Fulton County District Attorney's office, Bill Rankin, Beth Warren, Dr. Sanjay Gupta, Gord Downie, The Tragically Hip, Don Reynolds, Todd Reynolds, Lisa Rotondi, Xenia Rybak and Mark Holland. Condolences go to the families of court reporter Julie Brandau and Judge Rowland Barnes. About three weeks before their deaths, I met Julie in Judge Barnes' chambers to purchase a copy of the transcript from Dany Heatley's February 4 hearing. I asked if she thought I might be able to interview the judge for my book and, much to my surprise, after a few minutes she returned and pointed me down a hallway where Judge Barnes met me. He did not think it was appropriate, which I understood, and I appreciated that a person in his position and of his standing took the time to meet with me in person. I would also like to thank Emory University's library, theological library and law library and those at the Fulton County Courthouse who helped me to sort through the Heatley case file and make photocopies. (Apologies to anyone I might have omitted.)

I would like to thank people I consulted with about writing a book and getting it published, including Scott Burnside, Derrick Goold and Dave Bidini. I would like to thank friend and mentor Neil Greenberger for reading several chapters and offering criticism, comments and support. I would like to thank my friends for their support, encouragement and enthusiasm, including Carlos Frias, Sean Egan, Brendan Kirby, Dave Richards and Mike Sandler. And, of course, Mom and Dad, Lauren and Aly, thanks for everything. Thanks also go to the many musicians whose work put me in the right frame of mind to write, especially Buffalo Tom and The Lemonheads.

One note: this book is primarily about Dan Snyder. Dan's life, the events leading to his death and his family's ordeal will forever be inextricably tied to Dany Heatley, who was not interviewed. Because this book was written during the NHL lockout, I was unable to interview Heatley as a member of the Thrashers; regardless, his willingness to talk about anything related to the accident is extremely limited. I made several requests, through Heatley's agent, Stacey McAlpine, for interviews with Heatley, and I spoke to Murray Heatley directly about the possibility of being interviewed for this book. None of those offers were accepted.

Finally — but perhaps most important of all — I would like to thank my wife, Christie, for putting up with me during the hectic months of writing. I know during many late nights she wanted me to turn off the light so she could go to sleep, but suffered silently. Thank you for putting up with my stress during those days and nights when I counted the words I had written and calculated the number of days I had left before my deadline, which always sent me into a frenzy. Sorry for the times when I projected that stress onto you. Thank you for listening to me, taking care of Joey and Sam when I could not, thank you for your judgment, for taking time to read my drafts, your ever constructive criticism and your unending support. With love, you are my most trusted editor.

TABLE OF CONTENTS

CHAPTER 1

THE CRASH   *1*

CHAPTER 2

THE COUNTRY BOY   *17*

CHAPTER 3

THE CITY BOY   *35*

CHAPTER 4

FIVE DAYS AT GRADY HOSPITAL   *51*

CHAPTER 5

A FUNERAL IN ELMIRA   *73*

CHAPTER 6

THE FOUNTAIN OF MEMORIES AND THE ROAD TO HEALING   *93*

CHAPTER 7

"NOTHING LOVED IS EVER LOST"   *107*

CHAPTER 8

THE MENNONITES AND RESTORATIVE JUSTICE   *125*

CHAPTER 9

A RETURN TO THE ICE   *143*

CHAPTER 10
THE WOLVES *159*

CHAPTER 11
"HEAVEN IS A BETTER PLACE" *175*

CHAPTER 12
CARDS AND LETTERS *191*

CHAPTER 13
SUMMER INTO FALL *205*

CHAPTER 14
THE LAWYERS *217*

CHAPTER 15
RECKONING *235*

CHAPTER 16
CLOSURE? *255*

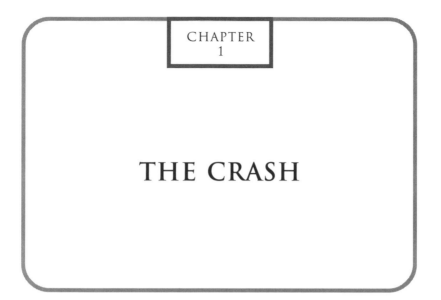

THE CRASH

Atlanta Thrashers general manager Don Waddell had made up his mind and decided it was time to deliver the good news. The start of the NHL season was three weeks away and even though Dan Snyder had not been able to take part in training camp, because he had undergone surgery on an ankle ligament, Waddell wanted the 25-year-old to know he had made the team. He approached Snyder and Dany Heatley, Waddell's budding star and the most valuable player at the previous season's All-Star Game. At Heatley's invitation, Snyder, a gregarious floppy-haired, gap-toothed player to whom teammates took a liking for his ever-present crooked smile, had been staying with Heatley for about a month, as Snyder had bounced up and down from the minor leagues to Atlanta and back during his previous three seasons.

"Are you getting tired of the hotel yet?" Waddell asked Snyder.

"No," Snyder responded, unsure of the line of questioning. "I'm staying with him," he added, motioning to Heatley.

"You've got to be tired of him by now," Waddell said to Snyder. "I think it's time to get your own place."

On that late September day, in oblique fashion, Waddell signalled to Snyder that he had would be with the team for the entire season. It was the crowning achievement of Snyder's brief professional career. Snyder excitedly called his parents and his brother Jake to inform them of the news and started his housing search. But the celebratory mood would last only a few days.

The week before Thrashers' training camp was set to begin, Waddell had persuaded Snyder to have the surgery, explaining bluntly that, with Snyder's skating ability, he needed to be at top form to compete in the NHL. That Snyder needed the surgery, in Waddell's mind, served as a microcosm of the player's career — barely fast enough, barely big enough. Nonetheless, Snyder embodied the ethic Thrashers coach Bob Hartley prized: He was tough, fearless, and with a mouth that never stopped yapping, no one wanted to play against him.

Snyder had been through enough trials before, so the 2003 training camp need not be one of them. Based on his performance at the tail end of the previous season, Snyder had earned a spot as the team's third-line centre for the 2003–04 campaign — a season which held high expectations for the expansion franchise entering its fifth year. In previous stints with the Thrashers, Snyder had lived out of a hotel room beside the highway near the team's practice facility in Duluth, Georgia, about 30 miles northeast of downtown Atlanta. However, since arriving in Atlanta in August from his hometown of Elmira, Ontario, to prepare for the season, Snyder had stayed at Heatley's home in the city's upscale neighborhood of Buckhead. Heatley, a right winger who had earned about $8 million in his first two pro years, was coming off a season many observers believed would act as a springboard to launch a spectacular career. He could become one of the best players in the world at his position — perhaps Canada's next great player.

September 29, 2003, was a practice day for the Thrashers. Over the weekend, the team had played exhibitions in Raleigh, North Carolina, and Richmond, Virginia. After a day of rest on Sunday, it was back to work on Monday. Hartley and Waddell had trimmed the roster down to 22 players, the number they planned to start the season with. Only two pre-season games remained. The boot that Snyder wore as a protective cast on his surgically repaired ankle had been removed the week before, and he was eager to get back on the ice.

"He kept trying to convince Bob he'd be ready for start of the season, which was probably a little out of reach," Snyder's older brother Jake said. "I could see Dan playing with that [injury]." That was his personality: no injury was going to stop Snyder from achieving his goals. At a pre-season game against the Carolina Hurricanes the previous week, Snyder wore a suit, a dress shoe and a sneaker where the recently removed cast had been — although unplanned, the mismatched shoes were typical of the kind of goofy behavior teammates came to appreciate in Snyder.

After practice on the 29th, the players attended an event at

Philips Arena for season-ticket holders. The ownership group that had contracted to buy the team the week before was present, and the players were there to schmooze fans and sign autographs. Heatley and Snyder were among the last players to leave, around 9 p.m. They got in Heatley's black 2002 360 F1 "Spider" Ferrari and headed for The Tavern at Phipps, a player's hangout not far from Heatley's home. At 9:47 p.m., Heatley and Snyder ordered 10-ounce draughts of Bass Ale with dinner, according to a statement bartender Greg Greenbaum later gave investigators. Snyder spoke to his former teammate Jarrod Skalde on his cell phone, confirming plans to get together the next day and attend an Atlanta Braves playoff game. The check came at 10:11; the players paid and left. Heatley turned left out of the parking lot onto Peachtree Road, then turned right onto Lenox Road to head home.

The details of what happened next might never be fully known.

The 2002 360 F1 Spider can go from zero to 62 miles per hour in 4.5 seconds. Its engine can deliver 400 brake horsepower — almost triple that of a Honda Accord — and it has a top speed of 180.2 miles per hour. It is made of a light aluminum alloy and weighs about 3,000 pounds, about 1,000 pounds lighter than a Ford Explorer. More a collector's item and an engine of speed than a utilitarian automobile, Ferraris are scarce, and keen-eyed buyers gobble them up quickly, as only about 1,000 are sold new in the United States each year. Unlike most cars that depreciate the instant their owners drive them off the lot, Ferraris appreciate because of their scarcity. Just over three months before that fateful September night, Heatley had paid $240,823 for the vehicle — in cash.

The car's previous owner, Steve Pruitt — a former professional race car driver — was later questioned by investigators about its speed. "Well, it . . . it . . . it's fast," he said. "I guess it just depends on your ability to be able to drive it the way, you know, the way it's capable of being driven. Obviously, you know, I . . . I . . . I drove competitively for four years, you know, so I . . . I kind of know how to handle a car like that." The investigator asked if a buyer was required to take special classes before operating the Ferrari. "No, no, no, no," Pruitt responded.

On the night of the 29th, when Heatley turned down Lenox Road, a narrow, sloping, curving byway overburdened by its present status as a commuter thoroughfare, he soared past the posted speed limit of 35 miles per hour. Later, the fastest speed his lawyer would admit to was 58. Two other forensic experts put the car's speed at more than 80 miles per hour — numbers whose ultimate reliability might not have stood up to scrutiny at trial. The Ferrari's speed proved catastrophic. For some reason, Heatley swerved abruptly to his left. Unable to control the car, he braked and lost control. The car's right rear tire skidded out in front of the right front tire as the car crossed the double yellow line and careened off the road. It slammed into a wrought iron fence with brick pillars. Air bags deployed. The impact obliterated one of the 4,400-pound pillars.

The pillar ripped the car into two pieces, and Snyder was ejected 12 feet from the vehicle, as his seatbelt was shorn. Debris lay everywhere. Heatley suffered a multitude of injuries: a concussion, a broken jaw, torn knee ligaments, contusions to his chest. But none were as serious as those suffered by Snyder, who lay unconscious on the pavement with a five-to-six-inch laceration on his head. He would never regain consciousness.

Amid clouds of dust and gas, William Cassino made his way to the scene. The security guard's shift had begun at 10 p.m., and from his vantage point at the guard house at The Plantation at Lenox, the condominium development whose fence Heatley struck, he later recounted hearing a "boom, boom, boom" — the sound of the Ferrari slamming into three separate brick pillars. He also said he saw Snyder thrown from the car. As Cassino walked bewildered and panicked towards the scene, he grabbed a portable telephone and dialed 911 at 10:22 p.m. Confusion reigned.

"Yeah, I want to report a bad accident on 3033 Lenox Road," he said.

"Anybody injured?" the operator asked.

"Uh, yeah, it's a man out in the street."

"He's out in the street?"

"Yeah, he's in the street. He — he was on a motorcycle."

"Hold on for the ambulance. I got an officer on the way. Hold on for the ambulance."

"Okay. Oh, man."

"I got the accident on Lenox, y'all."

"Oh, man, these people are dead."

"Who's dead, sir?"

"They dead. They dead out in the street on Lenox. Hurry up."

A second operator came on line. "Fulton County 911, what's the address of the emergency? Hello?"

"Hey, Fulton, we need y'all to respond to ah . . ."

"In a hurry, in a hurry," Cassino implored.

"Sir, calm down."

"Hello?" the second operator intervened.

Cassino called out to a bystander: "Hey, they need help. Quick, quick. They dead."

"At — he's at 3033 — sir? Sir?"

Cassino called out again, "Yeah, I got them on the phone now. Yeah, I got them. I got them on the line now."

The operator needed Cassino's attention. "Please speak to the ambulance, please."

The operator appeared confused. "Sir, what's going on?"

Cassino, who would later undergo therapy to get over what he saw, was in shock. "Oh, my goodness," he said.

"Sir?" the operator tried to get his attention.

"Yeah?"

"Tell me what's going on."

"I'm trying to keep the truck, the traffic from hitting them," he said.

"What's going on?" the operator asked.

"Um, they got . . . they done had a wreck and the car done exploded and they done fell out."

"OK, there's a wreck?"

"Yeah."

"The car exploded?"

Cassino was overheard talking to a bystander again. "Yeah, is he OK? He's moving? No."

"OK, sir, so he's not dead then?"

"Yeah, yeah, one is."

"One is dead?"

"Yeah."

"But the other one moved?"

"Yeah."

"OK."

"Sir?" the operator again tried to get Cassino's attention.

"Yeah."

"OK, tell me what happened."

"OK, they hit a wall in front of Plantation at Lenox. They need, they need an emergency vehicle here quick. The other one, badly."

"All right."

"Yeah?"

"How many vehicles are involved?"

"Just one. Just one. They ran into a brick wall."

"Someone was thrown out of the vehicle?" the ambulance driver asked.

"You can't tell it. It's all smashed up."

"What kind of vehicle was it?"

"I don't know. You can't tell. It's all smashed up."

"OK. How many people are in the vehicle, do you know?"

"Ah, just two . . . just two. Only two. The one laying in the middle of the street dead and the one on the curb."

"OK. Can you go out there to, to them and see if they're conscious and breathing?"

"No, one . . . one is barely, but the other is dead."

"Sir, she [the second operator] needs you to go and just, I mean . . . I know you say he's dead, but . . ."

"Yeah, there's people out here with 'em now."

"OK, is anyone's hand in the vehicle?"

"Huh?"

"Is someone's hands in the vehicle?"

"I don't know. You can't tell. The car is balled up. It's tore down. Ah, man."

"OK. Can you get close to the vehicle to see if the person in the vehicle is . . ."

"You can't. You can't tell. . . ."

"Nobody's in the vehicle?"

"No, no, no."

"So, there's a total of two people, correct?"

"Huh?"

"There's two people, correct?"

"Yeah, there's two people."

"They're both out of the vehicle?"

The two operators addressed each other. "They're both . . . they were thrown from the car. You got an emergency vehicle on the way?"

"Yeah, they're already on the way, but I need you to get close to them so that I can see what's going on with them."

"OK, one . . . one is move . . . he's not moving no more. And one is dead, OK?"

"One is moving?"

"Yeah."

"Is it a male or a female?"

"Two fe — two males."

"OK, are they conscious? Are they awake?"

"No, no, no."

"How old does the person look?"

"Uh . . . about thirty. About thirty. About thirty."

"And he is unconscious?"

"Yeah."

"OK, can you see any obvious injuries on them, like bleeding or anything?"

"Huh? He's not conscious. I . . . the emergency vehicles are here."

"They are there? OK, we can go ahead and let you go then. Hello?"

"Yeah, Fulton. Atlanta's en route."

The call ended. It was 10:33 p.m.

LuAnn Snyder talks about a preternatural connection she had with her son Dan, calling it a tangible physical presence. The first time Dr. Doug Adler of Grady Memorial Hospital called the Snyders' home in the heart of Ontario's Mennonite country, at 1:30 a.m., the phone rang five times and the answering machine picked up. The second time, the call woke up LuAnn Snyder, who sat up in bed and cried out, "Daniel!"

Dan's sister Erika had answered the phone, the news awakening terrible memories for her of a close friend's fatal car accident. LuAnn could hear Erika running through the house.

"Oh, my God, Mum," Erika said, as she handed her mother the phone.

"Your son has been in a bad accident — a very bad accident," Adler told LuAnn. "But he's alive."

He described the injuries and told her someone would be calling her for a presurgical consultation in 30 minutes. As she was asking Adler questions, a thought entered LuAnn's head. How could Dan have gotten into such a bad accident in his truck? She asked Adler.

"He wasn't in his truck," Adler said. "He was in a Ferrari."

LuAnn was speechless. Her heart plummeted. She knew he was with Dany Heatley. She fumbled for the words to ask if Heatley were alive.

"He's alive," Adler said. "He's ok. His injuries aren't as severe as your son's. He's conscious and alert. Your son is not."

LuAnn had trouble rousing her husband, Graham. She called her son Jake, who came over to the house. After waking up, Graham went over to his parents' home to inform them of the news, then gathered them for a vigil at his own home. By then, Jake was there, as was LuAnn's best friend, Marni. Several others were also present, including Graham's brother Jeff. The group nervously awaited news over the phone from almost 1,000 miles away. Graham, LuAnn, Jake and Erika made plans to take a 6:30 a.m. flight to Atlanta.

By the time Sergeant J.L. Hensal, an accident investigator with the Atlanta Police, arrived on the scene at 11:29 p.m., Heatley and Snyder had both been taken away, about 30 minutes prior, for treatment at Grady Memorial Hospital, about eight miles away. Hensal ordered that a blood sample be taken from Heatley at the hospital, under the Georgia Implied Consent Law, to determine whether Heatley was under the influence of alcohol. Snyder was admitted with a depressed skull fracture.

Hospital workers frantically attempted to contact Snyder's family members to obtain permission to operate. Doctors had trouble identifying Heatley and Snyder. LuAnn Snyder would later file a police report, as both men's driver's licences and some money had been stolen at the hospital. Nothing in Snyder's identification pointed towards his parents in Elmira. Randomly using Snyder's cell phone in the hope of contacting his parents, hospital workers reached the parents of one of Snyder's best friends, Ryan Christie, who played with Snyder for the Owen Sound Platers during their junior days in the Ontario Hockey League. Sherry Christie finally called the Snyders at 4 a.m. to ask why hospital workers had called her home — they could not inform her as to why they were calling. The following summer, Christie, who played with the Las Vegas Wranglers of the ECHL that season, would get married, and Snyder had been asked to be a member of the wedding party.

A few hours after Sherry Christie's call, the Snyders would meet up at the Toronto airport with Don Waddell, who had flown to the city for NHL general managers' meetings after the season-ticket holder event. He had just landed when he learned the news. At the same time, Heatley's parents, Murray and Karin, were alerted in Calgary, and in the early hours of the morning drove to the airport to be in Atlanta. Until they arrived, later in the morning of September 30, the Snyders and Heatleys had never previously met.

As the ambulance brought the injured players to Grady, a page went out to Dr. Sanjay Gupta — known to CNN viewers and *Time* magazine readers around the world for his medical reporting. Gupta is a neuroseurgeon at Emory University Hospital who works out of Grady, one of the Southeastern United States' leading trauma centres. He is on-call one day each week. At 2:15 a.m., Gupta performed a craniotomy to relieve pressure on Snyder's brain. As the wound was being closed, at about 4 a.m., Dr. Yi "Jonathon" Zhang called LuAnn Snyder with the prognosis. He was told that Dan came through the surgery well, but he had no way to tell how events might go from there. Dan Snyder was critically ill with a very serious head injury. Graham Snyder was told that until the family arrived, his son would not be left alone for one minute.

The Snyders left their home, about 70 miles from Toronto, at 5 a.m.

Because the accident took place in a busy, heavily populated area of Atlanta, onlookers gathered immediately and speculation began about the identity of the two men. Security guard William Cassino, who made the 911 call, assumed they were just "two rich kids." A television producer who lived in the area was on the scene, and sent a crew to Grady Hospital. Shortly before 4 a.m., Thrashers team president Stan Kasten read a statement that was picked up by a local television crew.

Some Thrashers players and staff members did not learn of the accident until morning. Around 9 a.m., they began showing up at the IceForum for the day's practice. As they arrived in their Hummers, Mercedes suvs and their trucks, they looked tired and distressed. They held a meeting and elected not to skate — an easy decision. Three members of the team were made available: coach Bob Hartley and two veterans, Slava Kozlov and captain Shawn McEachern. Asked about how the team could possibly concentrate on hockey — an exhibition game was scheduled for the following night at Philips Arena against visiting Florida — McEachern responded, "Nobody's really thinking about hockey. We're thinking about the guys."

As a 19-year-old, Kozlov had been involved in a car crash in his native Russia in which a passenger, his friend Kirill Tarasov, was killed. Perhaps out of deference to his two injured teammates, or simply too disturbed at the moment by painful memories, Kozlov chose not to answer questions on that subject. Hartley, a disciplinarian with a hard edge, met the press with reddened eyes.

Meanwhile, Heatley's agent, Stacey McAlpine, made it abundantly clear on Tuesday to newspapers in Calgary and Atlanta that "alcohol was not a factor" in the accident. If it had been, Heatley's difficulties with the law could only grow more acute.

Later on Tuesday afternoon, when Gupta addressed the media to explain the operation and Snyder's injuries, he rated Snyder as a "6 or 7" on the Glasgow Coma Scale, which runs from 3–15, with 3 being the worst. The scale is rated on "best eye" response, "best verbal" response and "best motor" response. Gupta also was concerned about "acceleration/deceleration," the kind of whiplash effect that killed NASCAR driver Dale Earnhardt. On the positive side, Gupta saw no signs that the brain was bleeding, which would indicate possible longterm damage. "It is a bone injury and the underlying brain looked good," he said.

While Dan Snyder was left to recuperate in the Intensive Care Unit under the assumed name of "James Johnson," Heatley was in a different wing under the assumed name of "Joe James Lewis." At some point during the night of the 29th, Heatley was charged with five counts: serious injury by vehicle, reckless driving, too fast for conditions, driving on the wrong side of the road and striking a fixed object. His leg was shackled to the hospital bed and his mug shot was taken, his face appearing swollen and bloated from his injuries. That picture would later become a source of acrimony between Heatley, his family and one of his hometown papers, the *Calgary Sun*, which ran the photo full-sized on one of its covers. With the regular season set to begin in 10 days — normally a time of optimism — one man was in a struggle for his life and the other had a lengthy battle awaiting with his own demons and with the law — much of it hinging on whether Snyder survived.

CHAPTER 2

THE COUNTRY BOY

Dan Snyder was at a crossroads.

As his life unfolded, September would often prove to be an eventful month. For one, it is the month when hockey training camps open.

In this case, it was 1995, and he sat in the stands at the Harry Lumley Bayshore Community Centre in Owen Sound, Ontario, pondering his future and facing a life-changing decision. For some teenagers, that decision might be which university to attend, to leave home far behind and venture to some unfamiliar and faraway place outside the security of family and friends. For others, it might be whether to join the military or to learn a trade.

With hockey his vocation, the 17-year-old Snyder's decision centred on whether to continue to try to play major junior hockey — the most competitive level in the Canadian leagues and, historically, the most traditional path to a career in the NHL. In his first two days of camp for the Ontario Hockey League's Owen Sound Platers, he had made a poor showing. The general manager of the team gave Snyder a choice. He could continue to try out and he would be given every opportunity to make the team. Or, he could go home and try to further his hockey career by playing at an American college or university, where his in-your-face style of play might have been discouraged. (The NCAA does not permit fighting and all players must wear full face-shields.)

The safe choice would have been to pack up and go home. Snyder was a good student and he could have pursued the scholarship angle — but there are no guarantees when it comes to being recruited for a scholarship — and playing two levels below major junior with Elmira's Junior B team would have made it harder for him to get noticed. Snyder's hand was being forced as a result of one of many NCAA regulations regarding amateurism. Because major junior players receive a small stipend from their teams, the NCAA deems players in those leagues — in Snyder's situation, the OHL, but also the Quebec Major Junior Hockey League and the Western Hockey League — to be professionals. As a testament to the NCAA's ability to micromanage, the rules permit players to attend a major junior camp for no more than 48 hours. One second longer and, in the NCAA's eyes, those players cease to be amateurs and forever forfeit the opportunity to play in their leagues — even if the player in question does not make the junior team for which he has tried out. In some cases, a scholarship can be worth as much as $40,000 or $50,000 (U.S.) per year.

On that fateful day in 1995, Snyder's 48 hours were up. "I can very clearly remember meeting with the general manager of the team, Rob Holody and Dan," Graham Snyder said. "I gained a lot of respect for Rob the way he handled it." Graham quoted Holody, "'From our standpoint, if I had to be making a choice based on last night's intrasquad game, you'd be packing your bags and going home. But I like the things I've seen in the past.'" Holody put Snyder's chances at 50/50 as to whether he thought Snyder would make the team.

Holody allowed Snyder to take Sunday afternoon to watch an intrasquad game and gather his thoughts. Holody was stretching the NCAA rules a tad as the small, skinny young Snyder tried to make up his mind. A year earlier, he had been 5-foot-7 and weighed 135 pounds and barely made the Junior B team in Elmira coached by Graham's brother Jeff (Dan was the final pick). Sitting in the stands next to Dan, Graham liked the situation with the Platers and thought it might be his son's best option. Owen Sound, with a population of 30,000, was the second-smallest city in the OHL. It offered the familiar setting of small-town life, like Elmira — unlike teams in metropolises like Toronto and Ottawa. It also was only a 90-minute drive from his parents' home, in contrast to a place like Sault Ste. Marie, which would have been an eight-hour drive north. "He was really undecided," Graham said. "I personally thought he should play major junior. I liked his chances better."

Hockey would always be a major factor in the lives of Graham Snyder and his family. For one, that's how he and LuAnn met.

Twenty-four years before Dan was drafted by the Owen Sound Platers in the seventh round, Graham Snyder was drafted in the same round to play in the OHL by the Oshawa Generals, one of the most storied franchises in the Canadian junior leagues. But in those days, the OHL only had 10 teams, instead of 20, as it is presently constituted. Having played goalie until the age of 13, Graham, a left wing when he was drafted, said his skating skills lagged several years behind those of his competitors'. So in his first tryout with the Generals, after he failed to make the team, Graham returned to Elmira to finish his high school education and play for the local Junior B team.

The next year, he returned to the Generals camp and again failed to make the team. At 17, the same age as his son Dan when he embarked on his own career a few decades later, Graham had completed high school and chose an assignment with the Generals' Tier II affiliate in Chatham, two hours away. Located in Southwestern Ontario about 45 minutes from Detroit, Chatham was where LuAnn grew up. One of her neighbours was the future baseball Hall of Famer Ferguson Jenkins. But while baseball was bigger in Chatham than it was in other parts of Canada, LuAnn grew up in a hockey family.

Both of her brothers played hockey, and the father of her best friend, Jane Anne Pletsch, held the status of a local celebrity. Fred Pletsch was a prospect for the Boston Bruins and played parts of three seasons for their minor-league team in Hershey, Pennsylvania. His best season for the Bears was 1954–55 when he had 13 goals and 19 assists, and 50 penalty minutes in 60 games. But with only 120 jobs available at the time, the NHL was hard to crack. Players could make good money coming home and earning a living while playing Senior A hockey, for which they received a portion of the profits while holding down a cushy job secured by a local company or official happy to help out a Senior A player. Pletsch — who spent his teen years in Elmira — was a member of the Chatham Maroons in 1960 when they won the Allan Cup, which is given to Canada's top senior amateur team. LuAnn still remembers her father's grainy eight-millimetre films of the Maroons' Allan Cup games. (The year before Pletch's Maroons won it, the Allan Cup went to the famed Whitby Dunlops, a team on which current Boston Bruins President Harry Sinden played. That Whitby Dunlops team represented Canada in the 1958 World Amateur Hockey Championships, where it defeated Russia, earning much of its lustre.)

As a teenager, LuAnn went to the Chatham junior team's games, where eventually she was introduced to the boy from Elmira. After his time in Chatham, Graham brought LuAnn back east, and their son Jake was on the way. But Graham still did not give up playing hockey seriously until he was almost 30. The game would continue to play an important role in his life through his children. Graham played hockey all over Southwestern Ontario. He played junior in Niagara Falls in 1974–75, where one of his teammates was future NHLer Willi Plett (the former Atlanta Flame retired in Atlanta's northern suburbs), then played senior hockey in Stratford. (In Niagara Falls, his coach would occasionally hold "fighting practice" where Graham learned a technique he would later pass on to Dan. During these "practices" players were instructed to grab their opponent's jersey near the armpit with their right hand to help block punches while keeping the other arm free to throw. The problem is that the technique only works if the opponent is right-handed.) Jake, Dan and Graham were all playing hockey the final year that Graham played competitively. "I was making $60 per week playing Senior Hockey," he said. "At some point in your life you have to decide how you're going to raise your family. It was a little too much."

So Graham channelled his love for the game into his boys: Jake, a goalie, and Dan, a forward. Having felt that playing goalie for too long stunted his own development as a forward, Graham was determined not to let the same thing happen to Dan. When Dan, emulating his brother, wanted to play goalie when he first began playing minor hockey, Graham told him a white lie to change his mind.

"We told him the local minor hockey association had a rule that only one player from each family could play goalie," Graham said with a devilish chuckle. Thus, a forward was born.

Although he was very involved in his boys' hockey careers, Graham said he did not do much in the way of on-ice coaching or drilling. "Jake and I were a little too much the same in personality," Graham said with a laugh. But Dan took his temperament a bit more from his mother and, much like his outlook on life, Graham had a benevolent view of coaches he instilled in Dan. While some parents rant at coaches for not playing their children enough, Graham, who would become general manager of Elmira's Junior B team, sought to infuse a healthy dose of personal responsibility in his son. "Dan and I tended to talk more about attitude than we did about specific skills," Graham said. "Some people think, 'Coaches are out to get my kid.' Very early on, I tried to instill in him that it was his responsibility. The coach won't make his decision based on, 'I don't like you.' Give the coach what he needs and what he wants for the team. I gave him tips on winning the coach over. Let the coach know you always want to be out there. Be looking at the coach when he has to make a decision as to who to put on the ice. Look him right in the eye. That worked in the pro ranks, too. I talked to him about the things you can control and the things you can't control. It's like a poker hand. A coach has to play the hand he's dealt. He was pretty good at doing that. I tried to pass on — I know it's a cliché — that it is a game and play the best you can. Don't cheat yourself. Don't wake up five years from now and say, 'I wish I had done that.' Never be afraid to fail. If you're the goat, so be it."

It was advice that Dan took to heart. Nonetheless, his hockey career was filled with near-misses. In 1994, as a 16-year-old, Snyder was one of the last players selected for Elmira's Junior B team. The decision to put Dan on the team caused controversy with at least one parent, who made an accusation of nepotism against the coach — Jeff Snyder, Graham's brother. "With [Dan], the talent thing wasn't the big thing," Graham said. "Locally, he wasn't the best player skill-wise." Later the coach of the Kitchener Rangers in the OHL and of Canada's paralympic hockey team, Jeff Snyder had to have a talk with his nephew after a sluggish start to that '94 season, informing him he was at risk of being replaced. The pep talk worked. By Christmas, Dan was playing better. He earned himself the Sugar Kings' rookie of the year award, and his uncle an apology from the parent whose son had been cut in favour of Dan.

Similarly, the following fall, when Dan's tryout with Owen Sound was faltering and his chance at the big time and the OHL was in doubt, he came through again. Rather than play it safe and go home to Elmira, Dan elected to go for broke. In fact, that day watching the Platers play an exhibition game against Barrie, while talking over the decision with his father in the stands of Owen Sound's rink, Dan had already made his choice. So confident was he that he would make the team before tryouts had begun, he did something of which his parents were unaware: he had packed his bags and brought them with him.

"For me, I think, it was one of the defining moments when Dan became a man, because he had to take responsibility for his decisions and what he wanted to do," Graham said. "Halfway through the game, he said, 'I'm going to play hockey here.' I thought, 'He's going to make this team.' There was no looking back. He led the team in scoring in the exhibition season."

Dan Marr is not one of those people who had an easy path to success in the hockey world — maybe that is why he found Dan Snyder so appealing. Balding and paunchy with glasses and a moustache, Marr, the Atlanta Thrashers director of amateur scouting and player development, hardly looks the part of ex-NHL player, as scouts often are. In fact, he is not. Instead, he took an unusual route from trainer into the world of an NHL front office. For five years, he worked as the trainer for the OHL's Toronto Marlboroughs. In 1986, Marr caught on as a trainer with the Toronto Maple Leafs and worked in that capacity for three seasons. (In one of the classier touches around the NHL, the Leafs have the names of players and their coaching staffs from every season of their existence on plaques that hang in the team's dressing room at the Air Canada Centre, and Marr's name appears on them for those three seasons.) In 1989, Marr became a scout for the Leafs. Nine years later, his path would intersect with Dan Snyder's, and Marr would become one of the pivotal people in Snyder's ascension to the NHL.

Marr's role is to identify players the NHL team would want to draft or sign. Once a player is the property of the Thrashers, Marr is their primary contact with the team. He tries to make sure they remain on track for the NHL, supporting them in whatever way necessary — or, sometimes, giving them a kick in the pants to tell them how they need to improve. Like most scouts, he conducts in-depth interviews with players the team is interested in selecting. On draft day, after a player is chosen, he acts as the team's liaison and lends a comforting and helping hand in the often bewildering hours that can represent the apex of the 18-year-old's life. As prospects' careers progress, Marr is occasionally there to shepherd them through the team's farm system.

Marr left the Maple Leafs in September 1998 for a promotion to head scout with the expansion Thrashers. Atlanta would join the NHL the following season, and after being awarded a franchise by the league, the organization had to start preparing for the 1999 draft and to start stocking its farm system. By then, Dan Snyder was 20 and entering his final year of junior eligibility. He had already gone through two NHL drafts without being selected, and going through the draft once without being picked can result in an unofficial blacklisting in the scouting fraternity. So once again, Snyder's hockey future was at a crossroads.

Marr says every time he watches a game he asks himself two questions: "Who is the best player on each team and who is the best prospect on each team?" After watching Dan Snyder for three seasons with the Platers he had come to a conclusion. "Every time," he said, "it was Dan Snyder. On the ice, he was willing to do what needed to be done. If he had to mix things up, he would do it."

One particular incident stood out. Marr was present one night when Snyder was cross-checked in the throat, his opponent breaking his graphite shaft across Snyder's neck. The Snyders still have the play on film — Owen Sound included it in a highlight video for them. "The guy cross-checked him right in the throat," Marr said. "Good God, I thought, is he going to have problems. He went down in a heap, but he wouldn't let the trainer help him. He came right back out. He didn't miss a shift. When you see little things like that, you get a sense of what the guy's all about and what he's made of. I would leave games knowing he's the best player. Those personal attributes, those are the guys you want to succeed. I knew I'd never be in the wrong by pushing him or promoting him."

Marr had first become interested in Snyder while he was working for Toronto and Snyder had attended a prospect camp with the Maple Leafs. Snyder was one of a select few players from the prospect camp who had earned an invitation to the Leafs' main training camp. By then, Marr had already said yes to his new job with Atlanta, but Toronto's front office wanted him to stay until the end of his contract and help run their camps. A team that is often top-heavy with highly paid veterans, the Maple Leafs had little room for marginal prospects like Snyder. Dan was not offered a contract, but he still had a memorable exit interview with then coach and general manager Pat Quinn. "One thing everyone commented was that Dan had big hands," LuAnn Snyder said, recalling the conversation her son had relayed between himself and Quinn. After shaking hands, Quinn commented, "'That's quite a paw you've got there.'" "'But, mom,'" LuAnn continued, "'they weren't as big as his.' They knew he was undrafted, and they said they would continue to watch him in Owen Sound. But

Snyder told Quinn, 'You haven't seen the last of me. You'll be seeing me in the NHL.' 'I don't doubt you,' Quinn said. [Dan] said his piece. He wasn't afraid to. He wasn't a smart mouth. He just told him he'd be back."

Ryan Christie said Snyder clung to that dream. Christie departed Owen Sound in 1998 and played in the IHL when Snyder played his overage year. Most undrafted overage players are making plans to attend university by then, or planning on playing in the ECHL, North America's Class AA league. But not Snyder. "People would ask Dan and he would say, 'I've still got this dream,'" Christie said. "'I'm still going for it.' He wasn't upset. He was pretty realistic."

Marr's impending situation with the Thrashers presented a bit of an ethical dilemma: He was still obligated to continue to look out for Toronto's interests while knowing he was soon leaving for Atlanta. After the Leafs failed to offer Snyder a contract, Marr simply told Snyder, "Better things are coming." Snyder was grateful. "'The only reason I was with the Leafs was [because] I was with you, and I'm going to stick with you,'" Marr recalled Snyder telling him. "He was a dependable and loyal guy."

Snyder attended the Thrashers' inaugural prospect camp in Traverse City, Michigan. He made an impression. On July 6, 1999, Snyder signed with the Thrashers, and became the long-shot story Marr uses each season at the Thrashers' prospect camp to motivate undrafted players. But he was still a long shot to make the NHL.

Mischief. That's the word Dan Marr uses to describe the way

Dan Snyder played; his "game," so to speak. It turns out the word was a metaphor for Snyder's personality as a whole. LuAnn Snyder recalled an incident from when Dan was in fifth grade. He had come home from school for lunch and, shortly beforehand, she had received a call from the school's principal. It seemed that two friends had cooked up a scheme with Dan to moon their classmates onstage during a school show. The ringleader and the other cohort chickened out, but not Dan. When LuAnn started digging around as to what had happened earlier that morning, Dan feigned ignorance. So she had to confront him with the news of the phone call. "It's not my fault," was his indignant reply.

"He was a leader but he could easily be talked into things," LuAnn said. "I was trying not to laugh."

Yet in other ways — ways he demonstrated first in the IHL, and then in the AHL in helping lead his teams to consecutive league championships — he could be a leader. LuAnn recalled how, as a sixth-grader, her son planned three years in advance how to win a school award for all-around student, athlete and citizen. As a fifth-grader, Dan started a recycling program for his school, then, the following year, a hot Christmas dinner for student organizations — a sort of holiday celebration — the Elmira school continues to this day.

When he made the Owen Sound team, Dan patterned his behaviour during his rookie season after the captain. That behaviour helped Snyder to become the team's captain during his final two seasons. In Owen Sound, he was charged with the responsibility of calling around to make sure his teammates made curfew. When he would call coach Dave Siciliano to give his report, their phone calls would often last an hour, just talking hockey. LuAnn said others have told her similar stories. "I've had so many people tell me that he could talk the birch off a tree," she said. "[Thrashers veteran] Jeff Odgers said he used to sit beside [Dan] because he enjoyed being around him." Many who knew him talk of how they were drawn to Snyder for the same qualities that appealed to a budding superstar like Dany Heatley. If people wonder what made an All-Star Game MVP offer his home during training camp to a player who had just made his first NHL roster at 25, this was it.

It was these kinds of quirks that also endeared Snyder to Dan Marr. Marr is from the small Ontario town of Dunnville in the Niagara peninsula, and could easily relate to Snyder. He got a kick out of the idea that one of Snyder's summer jobs during his junior days was working in a factory that made food for pigs. Snyder had had to sit atop a landfill and make sure stale loaves of bread and other old food were fed properly into a machine that ground it up into small bits. Marr also chuckled at the idea that LuAnn, a woman, was a volunteer firefighter, a typically male-dominated field in a small town. Marr still calls LuAnn on Mother's Day, and Dan's birthday in February, and attends baseball games of a team Graham coaches in the summer.

"I don't spend as much time with players as I did with Snydes," Marr said. "All the contact I had with Dan, he relayed everything I said through [to his family]. By extension, that keeps my relationship with Dan going."

In his first season in the minor leagues, Snyder had 12 goals and 13 assists in 71 games for the Orlando Solar Bears of the

IHL — not exactly the kind of credentials that would earn one a spot on an NHL roster. But his toughness was among his greatest attributes, as he played at times with his left index finger broken in four places. That summer the Thrashers put him on a nutritional program to help him gain weight. But with his metabolism, it was hopeless. He protested to his mother that he would have to stay awake for 20 hours and eat five meals a day to consume the number of calories it prescribed. His second season, he had one more goal but 17 more assists and showed himself as a defensive presence with a plus-8 rating. But his most impressive statistics — the ones that the Thrashers hoped would foretell the kind of player he would become — came in the playoffs. He had seven goals and three assists in 16 games, as Orlando won the 2001 Turner Cup, the final IHL championship before the league folded after that season.

That playoff season was a painful one for Snyder. He weighed 172 pounds when the playoffs started. During the gruelling playoff run, he would lose as much as eight pounds during a game, but could only gain six back before the next one. The attrition took its toll. After the season, he weighed 165. Three months before the playoffs started, on January 19, Dan had torn his deltoid muscle in his left arm. He could hardly grip his stick, and by the end of the season the muscle was completely torn off the bone. Dan had numbness and shooting pain. Often, he would seek the advice of his mother, a nurse, on injuries, and they had considered having her travel to Orlando for the surgery after the season, but for logistical reasons, she did not. When he visited home during the summer, Dan complained of itchiness and soreness. When LuAnn removed the bandages, she detected a foul odour — a pocket of dried, infected blood decomposing inside his arm — and something else. Dan had a tattoo stencilled on his chest as an homage to the strength of LuAnn's father, who would ultimately succumb in his battle with cancer. The tattoo — an Asian character signifying strength — would later become an enduring symbol of Snyder.

That season was also the one in which Snyder made his NHL debut, playing two uneventful games. Ben Simon was one of Snyder's teammates in Orlando, and became one of his good friends. Simon said that whenever a player gets called up by the parent NHL team, teammates often feel a pang of jealousy. But not in Snyder's case. He said Snyder's teammates always recognized how hard he'd worked to get his call-ups. The following season, the IHL folded, and the Thrashers moved their minor-league affiliate to the Chicago Wolves of the AHL. In Chicago, Snyder's production increased, and his leadership skills continued to develop, as did his reputation as a big-game player. He totaled 11 goals and 24 assists in 56 games, a rate of .63 points per game, up from .55 the previous season. In the post-season, he helped lead the Wolves to the Calder Cup title, the AHL championship. He had seven goals and 10 assists in 22 playoff games, tying a league record with five game-winning goals in the playoffs.

Snyder had become the type of player who would reach the NHL through sheer effort: killing penalties, winning faceoffs, checking when needed, chipping in a little scoring, providing leadership and team toughness — characteristics that endeared him to teammates and coaches alike. Snyder was not the Wolves captain — that honour went to the team's long-time veteran Steve Maltais — but he was an important leader.

"He was a guy everyone gravitated towards," Wolves general

manager Kevin Cheveldayoff said. "Through the tough times he would be the guy to lead you through it. To have a guy on your team who wasn't drafted, beat the odds of signing, always have to work the hardest to put weight on, get bigger or stronger. He was always too this or too that. But he could find a way to do it all of the time. He was an inspiration."

Snyder played 11 games with the Thrashers that year, and registered his first NHL points: a goal and an assist. But on a team that finished dead last in the 30-team NHL, he began to make his mark in other ways. On March 23, 2003, at Ottawa — a game which his family drove seven hours through a snowstorm to attend — he was thrown out for retaliating with an elbow to the head of the Senators' Sami Salo. (As his father, Graham, once said, "You would never know Dan was a Mennonite by the way he played hockey.") On a squad with little team toughness, the play stood out. It was towards the end of coach Curt Fraser's tenure with the Thrashers, and Fraser was constantly frustrated by many of his team's shortcomings. A tough player himself during his 12 NHL seasons, Fraser loved Snyder's play. Earlier on the road trip, Snyder had tussled with the Rangers' Eric Lindros and held his own, despite giving away four inches and nearly 50 pounds. Snyder earned a three-game suspension from the NHL and a fine for the hit on Salo, but the play endeared him to the coach. In a meeting between periods with Fraser after the ejection, Snyder thought Fraser would chew him out.

"'Mom, I thought he was going to kiss me,'" was the way LuAnn recounted it. "I thought that was great," Fraser enthusiastically told his pupil.

The season also was significant in one other way: it marked Dany Heatley's debut. Heatley won the Calder Trophy, given to the NHL's rookie of the year, the first season the two would get to know each other. The following year, Snyder played 36 games in Atlanta. He made the team out of training camp, but the Thrashers could not afford another bad start coming off their disastrous third season. General manager Don Waddell ominously said in the pre-season that he did not want to start two and eight, implying Fraser's future would be in jeopardy. But the Thrashers could not win a game in their first 10, and Fraser's fate was sealed. While the whole team had struggled, Snyder was expendable. He was sent down on October 30 — one day before the Thrashers were due to play the Maple Leafs in Toronto, a game his family planned to attend. The setback was crushing, and one of the few occasions Snyder let himself get down.

"'You're smart enough to realize you shouldn't be the guy going down,'" Graham said Waddell told his son. "It was political."

Less than two months later, Fraser was fired and the team hired Bob Hartley, who'd won a Stanley Cup with Colorado in 2001 with the likes of Joe Sakic, Patrick Roy and Peter Forsberg. Hockey fans might not have known it because of the skill of Hartley's Avalanche teams, but his favoured style was one of blood-and-guts, from his days as a junior coach in Ontario and Quebec. Among Hartley's favourite players from his junior days were NHL tough-guys Gino Odjick and Sandy McCarthy. Snyder was just Hartley's kind of player, and Dan got a fresh chance with the team later in the season. He had 10 points in that 16-game span, as the Thrashers played the best hockey in franchise history — four games over .500 during Hartley's 39-game tenure to end the season. Snyder finished the season with 10 goals, one game-winner and one shorthanded, four assists and 34 penalty minutes in 36 games. It all but ensured that Dan would start the following season as the Thrashers' third-line centre. The franchise's fifth season was to be a promising one and the team had every reason to expect to contend for the playoffs. Snyder appeared to have become that rare undrafted player to make it to the NHL.

"Ultimately it's all up to the player," said Cheveldayoff, the general manager of the AHL's Wolves. "There's a reason why these guys get passed over [in the draft]. Maybe they were too small. But getting drafted or signed gets your foot in the door. After that, it's all up to the player. You see some good things, then it becomes 'God, I don't want to play against this guy.' He chops you. He's all over the place, he's on you all the time. Opposing teams start noticing, and play away from you. You know you're getting your job done. Again, playing in the NHL was not given to him. It certainly was earned."

CHAPTER 3

THE CITY BOY

Sometimes the progeny of a professional athlete can exceed anything the parent has accomplished. There are exceptions, to be sure, like Pete Rose Jr.'s many years of ignominy toiling in baseball's minor leagues in the shadow of his father, major-league baseball's all-time leader in base hits. But then there are the sons of ordinary-to-excellent pros who become transcendent. It is hard to know how or why it happens, but there is no doubt that it *does* happen. Maybe the parent, knowing what it takes to reach the professional level, serves as a sort of teacher/coach and can tailor their child's life so they can excel at their chosen sport. Maybe it's just natural selection at work, taking already good genetics and transforming them into something sublime. In baseball, take Bobby Bonds and Barry Bonds, or Ken Griffey and Ken Griffey Jr. In football, Archie

Manning has produced sons Peyton and Eli. In basketball, look no farther than Joe Bryant and his son Kobe. In hockey, junior phenom Sidney Crosby — whose father Troy did not play beyond the junior level — is drawing comparisons to the game's all-time greatest. Dany Heatley is another athlete whose father was a middling professional.

Murray Heatley never played in the NHL, but he did have a lengthy pro career. He signed with the Toronto Maple Leafs, after finishing with 67 goals in 86 career games at the University of Wisconsin, the school his two sons ultimately attended. Murray Heatley played two seasons in the minor leagues before catching on with the Phoenix Roadrunners of the WHL. The following season, he landed in the incipient World Hockey Association, playing his first of four seasons in the league with the Minnesota Fighting Saints. He scored 26 goals and had 32 assists in 71 games in his first season and played parts of his final two seasons with the Indianapolis Racers, departing three years before a 17-year-old Wayne Gretzky would arrive with the franchise.

Like his son, Murray Heatley was a right winger. But he was 5'8", 180 pounds. By the time he reached the NHL, Dany would grow to a dominating 6'3" and 215 pounds. Nurture and nature have both appeared to play roles in Dany's development. Murray Heatley finished his playing career in Germany. His final three seasons were in Freiburg, where he met his future wife, Karin. Dany lived in Germany until he was three, when Murray decided to end his hockey career and move the family home to Calgary.

Professional hockey scouts do not normally hear about a player until he is 16 years old, when he becomes eligible to be drafted by junior teams. However, some exceptional younger players can gain notoriety before that age in the Canadian media, trying to fill a near-insatiable appetite for hockey coverage of any variety. Dany Heatley was one such player.

In the 1997–98 season, Dany was a member of the Calgary Buffaloes, competing for the Air Canada Cup, the tournament held annually for the country's top midget team (now known as the Telus Cup). A favourite to win that '98 tournament, the Buffaloes were upset in the semifinals by host Sudbury and ended up placing third. Nonetheless, the team had four players who proved to be high-round draft picks in the NHL: Heatley, Ben Knopp (taken 69th overall by Columbus in 2000), Adrian Foster (28th by New Jersey in 2001) and Krys Kolanos (19th overall in 2000). With a team as talented as that, the Buffaloes were bound to get their share of press coverage.

And Heatley was the best of them. He totalled 90 points in 33 games that season, was the top scorer at the Air Canada Cup and was named the tournament's most valuable forward. "So from Midget hockey you knew Heatley was going somewhere," said Dan Marr, the Thrashers' director of amateur scouting and player development. "He was in that rare group."

After the 1997–98 season, rather than go the gruelling route of major junior hockey — twice as many games and exhausting bus rides, without the perks of attending a university — Heatley opted to play Junior A hockey. (The NCAA deems major junior players "professionals" since they receive a small stipend. However, teenage prospects wishing to preserve their eligibility for an NCAA scholarship can play Junior A, one level down, which the NCAA, in its hair-splitting wisdom, deems "amateurs.") That choice preserved his eligibility under the NCAA's rules. One NCAA school Heatley had his eyes on was the University of Wisconsin, where his father, Murray, had played. While playing Junior A, Heatley's star kept rising. In the 1998–99 season with the Calgary Canucks, he was named the Canadian Junior Hockey League's player of the year, after he scored 70 goals in 60 games.

Mark Johnson was an assistant coach for the Wisconsin Badgers during Heatley's tenure. Murray Heatley had played for Johnson's father — "Badger" Bob Johnson, the U.S. hockey hall-of-famer who won three NCAA titles at Wisconsin, coached the Calgary Flames, and later the Pittsburgh Penguins to a Stanley Cup title in 1991. (Scotty Bowman succeeded him in Pittsburgh, winning the second of two consecutive Cups in 1992, as Johnson took ill and eventually died of brain cancer in November 1991.)

Mark Johnson, the leading scorer on the 1980 U.S. Olympic team — the "Miracle on Ice" team — recalled the time his father recruited Murray Heatley. Murray Heatley was a member of a group of Albertans whom Bob Johnson had sought to play at Colorado College, where he coached from 1963 to 1966. Then Johnson took the job at Wisconsin, and had to persuade the players to come with him.

"He had to call all these guys from Calgary and convince them, 'No, we changed plans,'" Johnson said. "They're looking at the atlas and going, 'Where the hell is Madison, Wisconsin?' 'Get your map and find it. We start school on September . . .'" his voice trailed off. "'Get there.' A lot of them were good players."

Johnson said that while it was not a given that Dany Heatley would come to Wisconsin, the school was not a hard sell. "In the back of his mind once he got here and went around campus and his dad still had some really good friends around town, he saw the facility [the Kohl Center], saw what was going on first-hand and said, 'Whoa.'"

Heatley left his native Calgary for the first time in the fall of 1999 at age 18, enrolling at Wisconsin. His brother Mark also enrolled there after Dany left, following in the family tradition.

Johnson can remember how singularly special Heatley's talents were from the first time he saw the player practice.

"Some guys have these little things you can't teach. Dany possessed them," said Johnson, who played 10 seasons in the NHL and was once better than a point-per-game player with the Hartford Whalers. "His ability to shoot the puck, his ability to get the puck in the net. And probably, to his biggest credit, his love and passion for the game. He would sit around after practice, I would bring my kids down. He just loved shooting. He loved being on the ice. That was his domain. As Happy Gilmore says, that was his happy spot. He's a rink rat."

If Dany Heatley had established himself as a third- or fourth-round NHL draft pick by the time he left for college, his freshman year at Wisconsin vaulted him into the elite. Most players eligible for the NHL draft opt in when they are 18; otherwise, teams cannot select them until they are 19. But because of those pesky NCAA rules, Heatley could not declare himself eligible for the NHL draft at 18, or the NCAA once again would have deemed him to be a professional and he would not have been eligible to play for Wisconsin. But as all 19-year-olds are draft-eligible, the NCAA cannot govern whether an NHL team selects them. At that point, they can only tell a player he must move on once he has signed an NHL contract.

For Heatley, the decision not to opt for the NHL draft and to go to Wisconsin kept him on that upward track. He had 28 goals and 28 assists in 38 games as a freshman with the Badgers, who won the Western Collegiate Hockey Association regular season title that year. At times, Wisconsin held the No. 1 ranking among Division I schools in the United States. "His first year, he was outstanding," Marr said.

For North American players, whether the best track to the NHL is via the NCAA or Canadian junior hockey is a hotly debated topic. For Dan Snyder, the juniors proved the best route. Heatley likely would have succeeded at either, but university life offers a more comfortable lifestyle. NHL teams only hold a junior player's draft rights for two seasons before they must sign him to a contract. Otherwise, another team can draft him. In the case of U.S. collegiate players, the NHL team holds a player's rights until he graduates, which can be four or five years.

"A player can develop at either venue he's playing at," Marr explained. "Some guys are junior players — junior-style players — and for others it's better to get the extra time at the NCAA level. There's not the rush to develop in the NCAA that there is to develop with the junior team. They have four years to develop, whereas in junior you've got to make hay when the sun's shining. . . . I think it's a great life experience to go through a university. You get a more life-skilled person. In juniors, you're 18 and you're treated like you're a 25-year-old. The lifestyle is that of a professional hockey player, so you're robbing them of some of their youth."

The Wisconsin Badgers play in the Kohl Center, a sparkling 14,000-seat facility that would be the envy of some NHL arenas. Madison, the state capital, is a sizable city and sits only 75 miles west from the major city of Milwaukee. In short, a player of Heatley's stature quickly learns to deal with the glare of the media — if he had not done so already by the time he arrived. With other prospects, scouts might make it a priority to meet them early and interview them as often as is possible to make certain they are not wasting their draft pick. In Heatley's case, he was such a can't-miss prospect that Marr did not interview him until the month before the NHL draft in 2000.

"I didn't talk to Heater until May, but there's a trainer's thing that I use," said Marr, a reference to his pre-scout days. "You can watch a guy play — watch his his body language, his mannerisms — and you have an idea of the personality. So it didn't take long with what I thought Heater's personality was. People talk all the time. You listen. My thing with Heater, he was exactly what I thought he would be. . . . You know why all the guys wear hats when they come [to the rink] in the morning? It's so they don't have to shower twice. When I met Heater, he just rolled out of bed and he didn't have the hat. That's what I liked about him. He wasn't trying to put on a show because these NHL scouts were in town to meet with him."

When Heatley became eligible for the NHL draft in 2000, many figured him to be the first overall pick. In what appeared to be a setback for the franchise, the Thrashers lost the NHL's weighted draft lottery — despite having a 25% chance of getting the first pick, the highest of any team in the lottery. They earned that chance by having the worst record in the league the year before. But the winners of the draft lottery that year were the New York Islanders, who had just an 8% chance of earning the first pick. However, in another of a series of missteps by New York Islanders general manager Mike Milbury, the Islanders bypassed Heatley for goalie Rick DiPietro of Boston University. Never mind that the Islanders had spent their fourth overall pick three years earlier on another goalie, Roberto Luongo. But Mad Mike, as Milbury is sometimes known, liked DiPietro, and on draft day packaged Luongo — a future all-star and Canadian World Cup team member — with Olli Jokinen in a trade to Florida for Oleg Kvasha and Mark Parrish. That left Atlanta salivating with the second pick, which they promptly used on Heatley.

"Truthfully we didn't know," Thrashers general manager Don Waddell said of Milbury's decision to pick DiPietro. "We were in talks with the Islanders."

About 90 minutes before the draft was set to begin, Milbury told Waddell he had traded Luongo. He did not say he was picking DiPietro, but it was fairly obvious. That meant Heatley was left for the Thrashers. Waddell described his reaction as, "Holy" — then censored himself. "It was a total surprise."

That summer, Heatley got his first taste of what the NHL demands. He attended the Thrashers annual prospect camp in July at their practice facility in Duluth, Georgia. This is the time a motley group of collegians, junior players and some minor leaguers and free agents get their first look at what a strength-and-conditioning coach for a professional sports franchise demands. Chris Reichart held that position for Heatley's first prospect camp, which Ray Bear, a former member of the United States Marines, took over a few months later. Regardless of who is running it, younger players have seldom encountered such a regimen.

"He saw how much work was ahead of him," Marr said of

Heatley after that 2001 prospect camp. "He just applied him-self to being a pro. The second year [at Wisconsin] was huge. Then the next summer, before training camp, every player — and it was the same with Snyder — you can tell when they put in that summer, that makes a difference. That's when it was for Heater, the summer after his sophomore year he put in [the work] that made a difference. Danny Snyder put his in his first year after he turned pro."

Marr said it is difficult for successful prospects to realize they need to improve their strength to play in the NHL. "Better strength gives you more confidence on the ice because now you can win those battles and you get through and you have more space," he said. "If you never had to work hard to score goals or be the best player, it's kind of hard when you say, 'OK, I want you to go out and spend three hours a day [working out] now.' They think, 'Well, I've never done this before, so. . . .' They have to go through it. It's human nature. That's why we try to use the development camp to instill that. Our guys [Thrashers players] are around here and [the prospects] watch how hard they work. You come in in the summer time and see Kozzy [Slava Kozlov] here. [Prospects think] 'Why is he here in July doing this?' We just expose them to what it's like to be a pro-fessional. Then he puts them through the workout. Then he tells them, 'Guys, that's nothing.'"

Perhaps Heatley realized how much he needed to improve. Perhaps he did not want to spend a season like Thrashers' centre Patrik Stefan, the NHL's first overall pick in 1999 who debuted in the NHL at 18, then spent part of the season con-cussed and physically overmatched. Whatever it was, Heatley decided to return to Wisconsin for his sophomore season.

"I just didn't think I was quite ready for the NHL, yet,"

Heatley told the *Atlanta Journal–Constitution* at the time. "I felt that if I wasn't 100% sure that the NHL was the right decision, I should go back to college . . . . Any time an 18- or 19-year-old guy gets thrown into the NHL, it's going to be tough on him. Hopefully, I can get stronger and quicker and be able to make that step a little bit better next year."

Johnson, the former assistant coach at Wisconsin, may have imparted some of that wisdom on Heatley. Johnson said physical development was precisely what Heatley needed to compete in the NHL. And he said that what Heatley picked up at that summer camp, which he had to pay for himself because of NCAA rules, paid dividends later, even if perhaps it was subconsciously so.

"What he needed to develop and what he needed to do was take his childish, boyish body and start to become a man. And as he developed that, then it was just a matter of flowers or trees blossoming and growing," Johnson said. "With him, the sky was the limit. I think there's two things. There was a choice to come back his second year. We talked about it. I had been a pro player. You look at the pros and cons, and I think his decision to come back was a good one. And the second part to that was during his second year. I remember I had breakfast with him just before he came down to Atlanta [for his rookie year]. I said, 'You grew as a player this year.' Because there was a window sort of right after Thanksgiving and the early part of December and January where he struggled. And sort of like a little light came on like, 'Click!' More time in the weight room. More time conditioning. 'What do I need to do to get better?' For four or five or six weeks, it clicked in there, and he did it, and all of the sudden the latter part of January, he was up here," Johnson said motioning upward with his hands. "He was just at a whole new level."

Johnson explained to Heatley the pressure on young players to develop in the NHL. That is especially true for high-round draft choices whose rights are owned by bottom-dwelling expansion teams. Johnson cited the example of Heatley's teammate Steve Reinprecht, an Edmontonian who played four years at Wisconsin, who more than doubled his point production from his junior to his senior year. Reinprecht was offered a free agent contract by the Los Angeles Kings for $400,000, and was later included in a blockbuster trade with Rob Blake that helped Bob Hartley's Colorado Avalanche win the 2001 Stanley Cup.

"So we were sitting there at breakfast," Johnson continued, "and I said, 'Part of your growth happened this year because you went through adversity and there were people who were concerned for you, they weren't going to bench you, and you were able to go through and figure it out. And through that adversity you're stronger and now you're ready to go.' That was towards the end of the year. He would have made it [in Atlanta]. I told Reinprecht and I told Heatley — and I tried to convince [Carolina Hurricanes' 1999 first-round pick David Tanabe, who left Wisconsin after one season] and I didn't do a very good job — when you get there, you've got to be ready, because you've got one chance to make a first impression. And Dany was going to make it. But you wanted to make sure when he stepped up that he's ready to go. As it turns out, it worked out beautifully.

"And Reinprecht was no different. We convinced Reinprecht it was like an investment. If you come back, we have Heatley coming in, we're going to have a top team coming in. We're going to be one of the top teams in the country. You can take your stock and go from here" — again motioning with his hands — "to here in seven months. Where else can you do that? And so he did that and he blossomed, [Reinprecht] was the best player in college hockey; he signed a great deal with L.A. Got traded, boom, wins the Stanley Cup. So, heh, heh, you try to give these kids the information and with Dany, one, he listened, and two, he really made the proper choices. The way he did come to Atlanta. . . . Phew! He was ready."

In Heatley's rookie year, the Thrashers continued to be among the worst teams in the league. But at least by the franchise's third season, the team looked like it had a bright future. Heatley and Ilya Kovalchuk — the first Russian player ever drafted first overall — created a buzz throughout the league. It started in early September 2001, at the Thrashers' prospect camp in Traverse City, Michigan, when all of the Thrashers' games were sold out at the facility the Detroit Red Wings use for their training camp. Heatley did not disappoint. He finished the tournament with six goals and four assists in four games; meaning out of 12 goals the team scored, Heatley was involved in 10.

By Christmas, Heatley and Kovalchuk ranked first and second, respectively, in scoring among rookies with 29 and 27 points. Kovalchuk was chosen for Russia's Olympic team in Salt Lake, but Heatley was left off Canada's team — much to the chagrin of some critics. Heatley finished the season with 26 goals and 41 assists playing in all 82 games — no small feat for a rookie who had played in only 77 combined during his two years at Wisconsin. Those numbers helped him earn the Calder Trophy as the league's rookie of the year. He and

Kovalchuk were both far ahead of the competition for the award when Kovalchuk suffered a season-ending shoulder injury on March 10, forcing him to miss the final 16 games of the season. Kovalchuk still finished with three more goals — though 16 fewer points — as Heatley showed the more advanced knack at that young age for making those around him better. Veteran Thrashers centre Ray Ferraro, near the end of his career, could see the promise the two players held. "It's certainly apparent when they're on the ice that they both want the puck, and they're going to get it a lot," Ferraro told the *Atlanta Journal–Constitution*. "And when they get it, they shoot it. That's the mark of someone pretty special."

It was at training camp that season that Heatley and Snyder first got to know each other. Snyder had played two games with the Thrashers the previous year, but as two young Canadian players just three years apart in age, they found a bond. The team was roughly half European, and throw in married veterans with families like Ferraro, Bob Corkum, Chris Tamer, Tony Hrkac and Jeff Odgers, and it is not hard to see how they had things in common. After training camp, Snyder did not return to Atlanta until March 15. But he stuck for that final month of the season — except when he was called back to Chicago on Thrashers off-days to help with a playoff run.

"He just seemed to hit it off with Dany right away," Jake Snyder said. "It was funny, I remember being at my friend's place in the summer time, and we had been out golfing for the day and we were in his garage having a few beers. It was three in the morning, or 3:30 or something like that. One of my buddies said, 'I bet Heater wouldn't even talk to you.' So Dan says, 'I have his number right here on my cell phone.' He ended up calling him. My buddy talks to Dany and says, 'We just didn't believe you knew who Dan was.'"

By the following season, Heatley's ability was no longer a secret around the league. Canadian media, in particular, seemed enamoured of the idea that he might be the next great Canadian player. In his sophomore season, in a *Sports Illustrated* poll of 28 general managers, Heatley was selected as the player most would want to build a franchise around. And that 2002–03 campaign did not disappoint in terms of his break-out performance. In 77 games, Heatley totaled 41 goals and 48 assists — the exact same numbers Kovalchuk would achieve the following season in tying for first for the league lead in goals, while finishing second in points. In 2002–03, Heatley finished sixth in the league in goals.

Most impressive was a dominating second half of the season. Bob Hartley was hired as coach on January 14, and Heatley flourished, carrying the team at times. Heatley totaled 29 goals and 24 assists for 53 points over the final 41 games — a pace that would have made him the league scoring champion in both goals and points. Heatley announced his coming greatness to the league in the All-Star Game on February 2, as he tied Wayne Gretzky's record by scoring four goals. That was the day a national television audience in the United States first became acquainted with Heatley's soon-to-be famous gapped-tooth grin, which he flashed to the cameras in accepting the game's most valuable player award. The game seemed to propel his confidence, and over the remainder of the season, his presence loomed over the opposition, his 6-foot-3 frame seemingly omnipresent on the ice.

Yet even while accepting those accolades, he kept his humility. The first day of practice after the All-Star Game,

Heatley was given the day off. "It was a lot of fun," he dead-panned. "It was good to see my parents and have a good game. I was anxious to get back here." During this time, his friend-ship with Snyder — who had just been recalled from the AHL — was growing. In some ways, they were such opposites: one was one of the rising stars in the NHL, the other was just trying to rise out of the minors. One was the city boy, the other was the country boy. But they shared mutual interests, and their sport acted as an egalitarian bond.

Shortly before the All-Star game, Heatley and Snyder attended a concert in Montreal together. Team assistant equip-ment manager Joey Guilmet, a music buff, went to the Our Lady Peace show with Heatley and Snyder at the Bell Centre.

"I often think back to when we were walking back [to the Marriot Chateau Champlain], the three of us, me, Dan and Dany, it's a short walk," Guilmet said. "We were back with the band, and hanging out backstage and just talking with the band about hockey. We were like three kids and just so excited. We had to slap ourselves. We could hardly believe we were backstage. Now, every time I walk back I think of that. How happy the three of us were. It was a pretty cool time." Guilmet saw other physical similarities in the two. "Their teeth, number one," Guilmet said. "They're both character guys, but one's a star and one's a guy who sets an example."

Three days before the accident, Murray Heatley had a conversa-tion with one of Dany's former coaches about his son's predilection for fast cars. Maybe it was a dark omen. While Heatley was in Raleigh, North Carolina, sitting out a pre-season game with the Carolina Hurricanes, a picture of confident and carefree youth, his father was home in Calgary having a talk with Don Phelps, coach of the Calgary Canucks.

"You know, his dad was sitting across from me in my office on Friday, and he expressed his concern about Dany having this fast car and everything," Phelps told the *Calgary Herald*. "And we're just talking as two parents. I have kids, too, the only difference is mine don't have a Ferrari. He just said he was worried because that car is built for speed and it's not like Dany. It's just something that, as any parent, you'd have a concern . . . not to know it could come to fruition four days later."

CHAPTER
4

FIVE DAYS AT GRADY HOSPITAL

Graham, LuAnn, Jake and Erika Snyder left their home in Elmira by 5 a.m. and were in Dan's hospital room four hours later, on the morning of September 30. Despite Dan's physical state, the first time his mother spoke to him, his vital signs leaped. For as long as they could bring themselves to stay at the hospital each day, with only a few brief hours for sleep at the Omni Hotel in rooms provided by the Thrashers, at least one member of the family was always at Dan's side. The Intensive Care Unit held little room for visitors, and some days much of what room there was had been taken up by another family, with many relatives present, agonizing over the decision to end life-support for a loved one.

So the prospect of someone visiting presented two problems: the first being sheer lack of space, and the second, the increased risk of infection if many people were to drop by. Two of the first visitors were Garnet Exelby and J.P. Vigier, who went to see Snyder without the team's permission. Vigier was a linemate of Snyder's the previous year on the Chicago Wolves team that won the AHL championship, while Exelby and his family got to know Snyder and his family during the tail end of the 2002–03 season. The two players were called up together by the Thrashers and they and their families each stayed at the La Quinta Inn in Duluth for about two weeks. Vigier called seeing Snyder that night as "one of the hardest things I've ever done, seeing one of your best buddies in that condition. Probably one of the only things that could be worse would be seeing your wife or your own child like that." Exelby also described the mood in the ICU. "Obviously everyone was worried. It was almost surreal when I poked my head around the corner and I saw him. I wasn't too close. I just saw from a distance. It didn't really look like him. It was hard to believe how we got to where we were. Obviously, it was very emotional with everyone there."

Darcy Hordichuk was a junior teammate of Exelby's with Saskatoon of the Western Hockey League and a former linemate of Snyder's in Orlando and Chicago before Waddell dealt him at the trading deadline the previous season. He also visited that night. Playing for the Florida Panthers by then, Hordichuk was in town for the next day's exhibition game.

"It wasn't a pretty sight," he said at the time. "That's usually not the way you see Snydes. He's the joker in the room. He's the one always smiling, the one who keeps everybody relaxed." He also visited Heatley, saying: "He's only worried about Snydes right now and how Snydes might be doing. [Heatley's] in shock right now. He still can't believe after seeing the pictures of the vehicle that they're both alive. Somebody up top was looking out for them."

Washington, DC, businessman Bruce Levenson met Dany Heatley two weeks to the day before the accident. Levenson, who would later serve on the NHL's board of governors representing the Thrashers, was one of eight investors who contracted to buy the team, along with the NBA's Hawks and Philips Arena on September 15. The next day, he'd met Heatley at a press conference. Two weeks later, Rutherford Seydel, one of the other investors, a blue-blooded Atlanta lawyer married to Ted Turner's daughter Laura, picked up Levenson from his hotel and drove him to Grady Hospital before 6 a.m. to learn more about the situation and see how they could help.

The previous night, Levenson was at the season-ticket holders event with Heatley and Snyder just hours before the accident. He personally requested that the players stay longer to accommodate long lines of fans seeking autographs. He remembers one woman in particular holding a hockey stick, desperate for Snyder's autograph. The woman got Snyder's autograph. The juxtaposition of events shocked Levenson.

"The first thing I saw was a police woman standing in the room and Dany was asleep," he said. "The next thing I saw was that he was handcuffed to the rail. His leg was. I just sat there for a minute and he woke up. He looked at me and started crying, and he asked me how Dan was, and I told him Dan was banged up but I didn't know his condition. And then we sort of half-shook hands and half-hugged each other. He was pretty groggy and very banged up. He looked like he was in a very bad fight. He said, 'I don't remember what happened. I just know Snydes is pretty hurt.' It was clear to me he knew he had been the driver and he was upset. That was the extent of it. I just sat there with him for I don't know how long, a fair amount of time. He dozed in and out. I tried to talk to him a little bit about hockey . . .

"I have three sons. One of them is about the same age as Dany. It was pretty easy to do a 'There but for the grace of God go I or one of my sons.' I was sitting there looking at, really, a boy. He's kind of in a man's body. I'm very close with my sons. It just hit me. I felt instantly paternalistic towards him. I tried to relate to him as I might my son, as if my son was there."

The next day, Wednesday, October 1, the Thrashers went ahead with their scheduled exhibition game with the Panthers. So began a period in which the team succeeded despite uncertainty about their teammates' health. The rink became a refuge, the one place where the players did not have to think about the harsh reality hanging above them every minute. One of the secrets to that success was that Graham Snyder asked to speak to the team before the morning skate, providing an inspiring foundation for that success. Graham Snyder had read *Atlanta Journal–Constitution* columnist Jeff Schultz that day, and was inspired by what Schultz wrote. Here are some excerpts from that column:

> If you're Dany Heatley, you're not thinking about the money, the car or the jaw. You're not even thinking about an NHL season that will begin next week. You're thinking about Dan Snyder, your friend and teammate, and there's a

probability you will be thinking about him the rest of your life. . . .

Only Heatley can match Snyder's love for the game. Two years ago, during the NHL's Olympic break, most players bolted for rare winter vacations in Florida, California or the Bahamas. Heatley? He was seen lugging his equipment bag out of the practice facility.

'Where are you going?' he was asked.

'Back to Wisconsin to see the guys,' he said. 'Maybe play some pickup.'

He is that rare combination in pro sports of great athlete and great leader. Players look to him for inspiration, for leadership. Since he was a rookie, he embraced the role, the responsibility. How must he feel now?

We can't possibly foretell the future. But we know Dany Heatley woke up this morning and Dan Snyder is in a coma.

The physical wounds, we can see. The psychological ones, we can't. Some lessons, we learn the hard way.

Graham asked Waddell if he could speak to the team, and addressed the players as they were dressing. As general manager of Elmira's Junior B team, Graham was accustomed to talking to players before camp and after the team was selected, and then later if some sort of problem arose, but he had never attempted anything like what he would do that day.

"I remember I talked to them about Dan, about the fact

that he was a fighter," Graham said. "I told them he was going to make it. I remember talking to them about there being another guy who needed their help, their teammate which was Dany. . . . I was thinking, 'Yeah, you know what? Right now he [Heatley] needs as much help as Dan does.' At that time, the media could be really, really tough on him at times. [I told them,] 'We're a hockey family. I understand the hockey mentality and it's maybe a bit of a cliché, but Dan would want you to be playing because this is what you do, you play hockey.' They were just as upset as we were. . . . The best thing to do is play.

"I remember standing there and thinking how I didn't really know what I wanted to say. But I really felt strong for some reason — I don't know where that strength came from either. But I remember I have a tendency to kind of rock back and forth and fidget a bit when I'm talking to people in person, so I put my hands behind my back and spread my legs apart so that I wouldn't sway around. And I remember Bob Hartley saying to me afterwards walking out, 'I don't know how you can do that. You were like an oak tree there, so much strength.' I had to be just to talk, I guess, it just came to me that that would help me, and would help me collect my thoughts a bit, too."

Asked what the mood of the players was like when he arrived, Graham paused thoughtfully before answering. "They were very, very grim-faced. Very, very sombre, I guess. And I could kind of tell they were pretty emotionally on the edge. I don't want to be too melodramatic, but I almost felt like I was getting some strength from somewhere, and it was coming through me and you could see it was giving them some strength. 'OK, we're going to do this. Dan's going to do this, and we're going to beat this thing together, as a team.' I thought Bob Hartley did just a great job of taking those players and building the unity and the togetherness. Those guys I'm sure would've done just about anything for him at that time."

Many have talked about the role reversal during that time period — how the Snyders reassured others when it should have been the other way around. "It was a very reassuring voice that I think the players needed," Thrashers coach Bob Hartley said. "I think we needed it as an entire organization. Just to see him stand in the middle of the room and talk to the players, I thought, 'Where are they getting their strength to do this?' I don't know, but it was pretty amazing. The message was real simple but it was to the point. . . .

"We had a bond with the Snyder family and the Heatley family. I think we were working for them while they were working for us, too. I think both families appreciate what we were doing for them, but at the same time, maybe they were not realizing that they were helping us a lot, too. There was lots of uncertainty in our minds and lots of distractions, obvious distractions, for the right reasons. They kind of brought us to, 'Let's all do this together.' They wanted us to be playing hockey, but keep thinking about the two Dannys. Play hockey, try to have fun. And having fun was basically something that was practically impossible at that time."

After Graham's talk and then the workout, the players reflected the positive message. "It was good to be on the ice," defenceman Chris Tamer said after the skate. "You can't sit around and think about it all day." And that day coach Bob Hartley — perhaps picking up on Graham's theme — began the mantra of playing "for the two Dans."

"We have two members of our family who are not with us,"

he told the media that day. "They're in the hospital and it's tough. We hope to do our best to overcome this. Today, we're doing the best thing. We're getting on the ice. We had a good practice. Once the puck will drop, we'll play for those two guys. If we would ask both Dannys what they would want us to do, that's what they would want us to do."

Wearing tape on the back of their helmets with the numbers 15 for Heatley and 37 for Snyder, the Thrashers went out and won 3–2 that night. In what was the beginning of an amazing run in the face of adversity, the Thrashers did not lose a game — in regulation, pre-season or regular season — for nearly a month. Throughout the run, players would often credit Graham's speech for giving the team life despite the circumstances. For a five-year-old franchise accustomed to starting the season with long losing streaks — the previous year they had not won a single game in their first ten — the streak was dumbfounding. And then there was the way they did it. Some of the comebacks were of the near-impossible variety. Given the tragedy, it was doubly baffling.

For a while, Dan Snyder's medical condition also seemed to provide some reason for optimism. The injuries to Snyder's head showed a marked reduction in swelling on Wednesday. The medical staff remarked at Snyder's fitness, surely a positive in this instance. But unbeknownst to many, a troubling sign also arose that day — Dan had developed a fever. As a nurse, LuAnn Snyder understood the seriousness of what that could possibly indicate: infection.

Grady Memorial Hospital, a monolithic brick structure

that towers over Interstates 75 and 85, sits on the edge of Atlanta's downtown. A few blocks north of the hospital, the city is going through an urban renewal. To its south are many of the troubling sights of urban decay. Immediately bordering the hospital is a large public housing project — which was scheduled for demolition in 2005. In 2001 and 2002, the city of just over 400,000 averaged nearly 150 homicides. As a leading trauma hospital in the midst of such violence, Grady gets its share of stabbing and gunshot victims. So when LuAnn was told not to worry about sepsis — or infection — because Dan's injury was "clean" compared to some of the victims of violent crime the hospital's medical staff saw, it allayed her fears. But she also had an ominous conversation with one doctor whom she chose later not to identify. He blithely informed her — perhaps intending to show that his patients did not die from their trauma injuries — that nine out of ten of his patients who died, died of sepsis.

On Wednesday, Dan Snyder's fever passed.

There had been a good reason why the Snyders collected their immediate family back in Elmira when they'd first received the call from Grady Hospital. They knew the story would quickly spread to the news, and they wanted to inform those close to them before they found out on television. Despite intense interest in the events, the team tried its utmost to shield the players and their families from the media. On Wednesday, the Snyders released their first statement to the media through the Thrashers. It read: "We are humbled and overwhelmed by the support and prayers that we've received from all over, especially from back home. Dany Heatley and our son, Dan, need strong support and positive energy in order to be able to overcome the difficult challenges that lie ahead. The support from the Thrashers family, the doctors and entire staff at Grady Memorial Hospital has been outstanding. Both Dan and Dany are getting the best care possible. These two young men are in need of our prayers, and we thank you again for your thoughtfulness during this difficult time."

The statement set the tone for how the Snyders would handle the crisis, linking the hopes of their son with those of Dany Heatley — and not casting blame on Heatley or seeking legal redress. Reached that day by cell phone back in Ontario, Snyder's agent Todd Reynolds described what the family was going through: "They're experiencing every emotion under the sun," he said. And, again, in a revealing moment, he was asked whether the family was contemplating legal action against Heatley: "I wouldn't know at this point. They're just worried about the comfort of their son."

In fact, the family was anything but hostile towards Heatley. On the morning her family arrived, LuAnn Snyder was questioned by members of the Fulton County District Attorney's office. When informed that Heatley's leg was shackled to his hospital bed, LuAnn demanded that he be unchained before his parents arrived. By the time the courthouse opened on Tuesday morning, team officials had arranged to post the $50,000 for Heatley's bail. During those first few days when Heatley remained at Grady, members of the Snyder family would visit him in his room. When he was not sleeping, they would sit with him and play board games, each trying to comfort the other, a ritual that would continue over time.

After flying to Atlanta on Tuesday, the Snyders would wake to arrive early at the hospital each day. Before leaving the hotel for the hospital, one of the doctors on Grady's medical team would phone them at the hotel with Dan's vital statistics, so they would not have any surprises upon arriving. After the surgery, Dan's head injuries appeared to stabilize, but the doctors remained cautious in their outlook. While still unconscious, Dan had shown some positive signs. One was that he reacted to his mother's voice. In addition, doctors had to monitor his blood sugar carefully, as elevated levels are associated with worsening of neurological injuries. That meant constant pinpricks to his finger to obtain a blood sample. When the nurses came for the sample, Snyder would instinctively recoil his finger — a sign that he was aware of what was about to come.

By Thursday, Heatley was transferred to St. Joseph's Hospital, about 15 miles from downtown Atlanta, in the more affluent suburbs north of the city. Team doctors wanted to get a closer look at his knee injury, and to get to work on whatever surgery he needed. Meanwhile, the team was getting inundated with flowers and letters of support. With hospital policy preventing flowers at Grady's ICU, many were donated to charity.

As improbable as it might seem, those days did provide a light moment or two. The head of the nursing staff, Teresa Fields, gave the family massages to try and keep them relaxed. After the ordeal, LuAnn would remain especially grateful for the work and support of the nursing staff. One of those lighter moments came when the Snyders decided to venture out of the ICU to the hospital's cafeteria for the first time. Jake Snyder was wearing a Thrashers hat and team-issue T-shirt, when one of the workers behind the counter asked him if he knew of the high-profile hockey player who was being treated there. He answered that the player was his brother. The woman broke into an excited state and slammed down her ladle.

"Lord, I am just *praaaaaying* for your brother!" she exclaimed, almost managing a smile out of the startled Jake.

The story was emblematic of those days. LuAnn Snyder would remark about how many people she encountered — once they realized who she was — would tell her they were praying for Dan. And she always felt the sentiment was sincere.

Even before Heatley and Snyder's accident, general manager Don Waddell had talked about acquiring a scoring forward. On Friday, with the Thrashers badly in need of manpower, they helped themselves by picking up three players in the waiver draft. Serge Aubin and Ronald Petrovicky would become essential members of the team. Aubin, a versatile forward, had played for Hartley in Colorado and in the AHL at Hershey, and Petrovicky, a gutsy Slovakian right winger, played in the same division against the coach when Petrovicky was with the Calgary Flames. Curiously, the team also picked up Jani Hurme from Florida, giving them three goaltenders in a season when it appeared the two returning goalies — Pasi Nurminen and Byron Dafoe — would probably split time equally in net.

A few hours after the waiver draft, the Thrashers played

Nashville in their final pre-season game, winning their second in a row. Graham and Jake Snyder attended the game that night. At the time, they were not as recognizable as they would become in the coming weeks and months, after doing televised interviews on most major Canadian outlets and a few American ones. They had been holed up in the ICU for 12 or 14 hours at a time, and after four days, began to look for diversions. During a normal winter, Graham and Jake might play, or coach, or attend a game five or six nights a week, so they were also looking for a hockey fix. They knew a few players on the Nashville team — like Curtis Murphy and Ben Simon, Dan's former teammates — and wanted to see them play. But after arriving at the rink, they realized they had made a mistake. There were simply too many mixed emotions.

"We certainly weren't ready for that," Graham said. "Dan's in the hospital fighting for his life. These guys are out here [playing hockey]. Are we ever going to see him play again? Is he going to live? Just a little too much for even diehard hockey fans like Jake and I."

During the second intermission, in an interview session outside his box on the press level nine stories above the ice, Waddell apprised the media of Heatley's medical condition, revealing that an MRI showed he had torn the anterior cruciate ligament in his knee. In football, a player can require two seasons to recover fully from that kind of injury. In other sports, it can easily be a season-ender. Before advances in sports medicine, it was an injury that had ended many athletes' careers. So, because Heatley was facing so much uncertainty in regard to his legal situation and his medical situation — let alone his mindset — the team declared that he would be out "indefinitely." "We won't comment on a time frame," Waddell said. "Until you go in there [surgery], with these kinds of things, you never know." Waddell added that he expected Heatley to have surgery to repair the injury in a week to 10 days.

As for Snyder, Dr. Sanjay Gupta released a statement saying his condition remained unchanged: Dan was still in critical condition.

Late on Saturday night, doctors made Snyder's coma drug-induced for the first time so that he would no longer fight the invasive monitoring he was receiving. By Sunday, Graham Snyder felt safe enough, based on what doctors had told him, that Dan's situation had stabilized enough that he could return home to Elmira to tend to some affairs. He left the hospital at 3 p.m. By 5:30, doctors were telling LuAnn that Graham should return as soon as possible — Dan's condition had taken a turn for the worse.

LuAnn described "a scurrying and a flurrying" of doctors and nurses, constantly in and out of Dan's room. When she entered to try to find out what was happening, she had a hard time getting answers.

"Then all hell broke loose," she said. "It was just so tense. I'd say, 'What's going on here?' And nobody had any answers."

Dan had developed another fever, but unlike the one that passed on Wednesday, this one persisted. Doctors already were treating him with strong antibiotics. It was like trying to put out a forest fire with a garden hose. An infection had taken hold of Snyder's entire body and was attacking all of his major organ systems. After being implored by Dr. Grace Rozycki, one of the doctors leading the medical team, to "Get your husband back here now!" LuAnn called Graham with the news that Dan had taken a turn for the worse and promised regular updates. Summoned by a nurse to Dan's room in the ICU, LuAnn, Jake and Erika witnessed a chaotic scene. The instant they neared the room, Dan flat-lined. With the hospital chaplain, they formed a circle just outside the door and prayed loudly, repeating, "Come on Dan, you can do it, you can do it!" Doctors employed a defibrillator and CPR to try to restart Dan's heart. The anxious family members waited for a while, then returned to the family room. Not more than 10 minutes later, at about 8:30 p.m., Dr. Rozycki flung open the door to the family room and said, "He's gone. I'm sorry, there's nothing else we can do."

Jeff Snyder had picked his brother up at the Toronto airport and Graham was riding back to Elmira with Jake's girlfriend Dawn. He was less than 30 minutes from home. Knowing she had to deliver her husband the cruellest news of their lives, LuAnn's training as a volunteer firefighter kicked in. She called Graham on his cell phone and told him to pull over, before telling him of Dan's death.

"To call your spouse, that was the hardest thing I've ever had to do in my life," LuAnn said. "I would never wish it on my worst enemy."

On one of the first few days after the accident, Thrashers assistant public relations director Rob Koch gave LuAnn Snyder the watch Dan had been wearing the night of the accident. Dan never liked to wear a watch — he had won one as IHL rookie of the month with Orlando but had never worn it —

so LuAnn did not recognize this one. It was a silver Wittnauer with a metal wristband, and it was broken in three places: the face in one piece, most of the band in another, while a small link comprised the third. Taking it in her hands, LuAnn noticed the watch had some dried blood on it. Koch took it away, had it cleaned and returned it to her.

The rest of the week, LuAnn kept the remnants of the watch with her at all times as part of her routine. When she went to sleep at night, she would keep the face under her pillow. Sometimes she would wake up in the middle of the night, frantically searching for fear that she had lost it. The face had some scratches, but otherwise it kept perfect time.

That Sunday night, the Atlanta Braves had a home playoff game against the Chicago Cubs. At the time, the Thrashers were still owned by Time Warner, which was also the parent company of the Braves. Bob Hartley attended the game with 20-year-old Russian Ilya Kovalchuk, an employee of Kovalchuk's agent, and Thrashers videotape coordinator Tony Borgford, one of Hartley's closest friends with the team — "Batman and Robin," is what Hartley calls them. Hartley said they were sitting in one of the front rows, basking in good news. The night before, the swelling in Snyder's brain had relaxed to the point that for the first time since the accident, it was not touching his skull. He was greeted at the game by Rutherford Seydel, who asked Hartley how Snyder was doing.

Hartley said Seydel did not have a chance to sit down before the coach's cell phone rang. It was Thrashers general manager Don Waddell, who informed him — and he still remembers the words — "Danny didn't make it." Hartley immediately left for the hospital with Kovalchuk and Borgford. Turner Field is one of the places in Atlanta where

Hartley is most recognized, and as he was leaving he was asked, "Coach, where are you going?" He tried to hide his emotions so as not to give away the news.

"The last two days were two of the best days we had in a long time," Hartley said more than a year and a half later. "For me, it was a terrible shock."

In those minutes after Dan Snyder passed away, his watch would take on greater symbolic meaning, for his memory and for the Thrashers. "When he passed away — I can't remember the exact sequence of events — I went in [his room] and came back out," LuAnn recalled. "A few of the players were there. I'm pretty sure Shawn McEachern and Don [Waddell]. Bob had been in to see me. [Latvian team masseur Inar Treiguts, who served as Kovalchuk's translator during his rookie season] was there. There were two other guys. I'm not sure if Slava [Kozlov] was there. I went over and spoke to each one of them. The kids [Jake and Erika] were there. I remember going along one wall, and at the end of this wall where they were standing, I could see this guy leaning against the wall and his head was bent and he was crying. And I said, 'Who's that?' 'That's Ilya.' I had never actually met Ilya — never met him outside the realm of the arena. I didn't know that was him. I was told, 'He wants to talk to you.' We stood and chatted for a bit.

"I don't know what came over me to think of it. He said how much he's going to miss Dan and how much he's going to miss him as a person. He was a good friend to so many people. Ilya was quite distraught. I still don't know what made me do it. He [mentioned] a few times about how he would miss [Dan]. I took out the watchband and gave the piece to Ilya. I said, 'This is a link — part of Dan from a part of his watch that broke away,'" she said, breaking into tears in retelling the story.

"He's gone from the team now. He's gone from us. He's broken away, but I want you to have this to always remember him. It's the missing link. It'll be the missing link for this year. You're starting off without him. Do you understand?"

"Yes, I understand," Kovalchuk responded.

"He did understand what I was saying. Inar was there, saying, 'Yes, yes, he understands.' We talked for a little bit. Ilya said, 'Yes, yes, I want it.' I told him it's going to be hard. It's going to be a hard year. You have to work hard and you have to be a leader. You don't have to play for Dan, but be there for him. He said, 'Yes, I will do this and I will try hard, I promise.'

"Then I went over to Bob and we talked for a bit, and I told him what I did. I took out the band and gave it to him. I said, 'I want you to have this.' I think it feels more personal because it has been part of touching someone's body. 'I've given Ilya the link. Be the missing link for Dan this year. I'm going to keep the face. When the year's over, we'll be whole again. The watch will be packed together, and we'll be all together, and this will be behind us.'

"Every time I see him he carries it with him. He said, 'I will have this behind the bench at every single game.' We did see him at games. He'd reach in and show me. I carry mine with me all the time. It is always with me. The only time I don't take it with me is when I travel internationally. If I ever lost it, I'd be so beside myself. It's something I carry as a talisman of Dan. I always have pockets and I always carry it in my right pocket. . . . Thinking about it now and talking about it now, I can cry. So many people there needed comfort and support. I had to do that. Maybe it was that the mother instinct, to look after these people who were so shocked and distraught at the time, took over."

Later, her husband, Graham, would ask LuAnn what compelled her to do what she'd done.

"I just felt the need to do something. Everyone was very distraught. It was something I felt could promote some healing, and they would always have something of Dan's."

LuAnn's need to comfort others extended beyond the players. She took it personally that after Rozycki informed her that Dan had died, she never heard again from another doctor on the medical team. But from the neurosurgery team, Dr. Gupta visited the room.

"I'll never forget what LuAnn did," he said. "I walked in the room right after I found out Dan had died. I didn't know what to say. She just looked at me and gave me a huge hug. She said, 'I know this is hard for you, too. You did a wonderful job on Danny.' What presence of mind to even think of that, let alone say that."

The next week, Hartley had T-shirts made for the players to wear underneath their equipment during games that season. They kept the story behind the shirts mostly private. The back depicted the watch sundered in its three places. One shoulder bore the date that Dan died, the other, a tattoo of Snyder's — the one he hid from his mother — the Asian character signifying strength. The back of the shirt bore Snyder's number 37 and the words, "We're All In It."

"I always have it," Hartley said of the watch. "I always have it. . . . Mrs. Snyder grabbed me in a corner and said, 'I want to give you this. He loved you so much.' To find that strength, I was melting. She was as strong as — I don't know how to say it. I didn't know what to do. Every game I coached, this bracelet is in my pocket."

LuAnn also offered another explanation for being able to maintain her composure. As a nurse, she started asking the doctors what might have gone wrong: the medical side of her personality separating from her emotional side, as she puts it. Upon learning of Dan's death, her thoughts turned towards finding something positive that might come out of it. A proponent of organ donation, she asked if Dan's organs could be donated.

When she felt doctors did not act upon her request seriously, she began to wonder why. The medical examiner's report performed on Monday, October 6, listed the cause of death as "blunt-force craniocerebral trauma, delayed effects." Under "comment/opinion" the report read: "This 25-year-old white male died ultimately from blunt-force trauma to the head sustained in a motor vehicle incident in which he was reportedly the front-seat passenger in a car that hit a fixed object. Although he survived the immediate trauma, he eventually succumbed to the delayed effects of his injuries. The manner of death is an accident. . . ."

It continues, "The decedent was treated with broad-spectrum antibiotics and had negative blood, CSF and sputum cultures. None of the tissues examined demonstrated evidence of infection. Therefore, sepsis is an unlikely mechanism. . . ." And: "Neurologic factors are the most likely contributors to the mechanism of death in this patient who had sustained a head injury. This can cause shock and elevated body temperature, even in the absence of anatomic findings." However, in its final summation, the opinion did hedge a bit: "Mechanism is generally difficult to determine by autopsy and is not necessary for death certification. In this case, the mechanism is most likely neurogenic shock, although cardiac dysrhythmia and sepsis cannot be completely ruled out. Any of these mechanisms would result from the head injury, and any attempt to single out a mechanism would not change the underlying cause of death." The report pointed a finger at the team of neurosurgeons.

But LuAnn's thoughts kept returning to why her request for organ donation was "pooh-poohed," as she put it. For an athlete like Dan, it just did not make sense to her that his organs would not be usable. "I, not demanded, but insisted, on an autopsy," she said. "They were a little reluctant." The autopsy confirmed her suspicions. On a document headed, "Grady Health System, Eye, Organ, and Tissue Donation Checklist" the box "no" was checked next to each: "Eyes are medically suitable," "Tissue is medically suitable," and "Organs are medically suitable." Next to each line was a space that read, "If no, give reason." Sepsis was given as the reason in each case. The form was completed at 9:35 p.m. on Sunday, October 5.

In the end, at LuAnn's instigation, the cause of Dan's death was changed from the delayed effects of head trauma to septic shock. According to the Society of Critical Care Medicine, septic shock affects 750,000 people annually in the United States, resulting in about 215,000 deaths. It is the leading non-coronary cause of death in the ICU. Because Dan's medical situation was so precarious that week, and information was so tightly held, it was hard to gain an accurate picture from the outside as to whether he would have survived the crash. But not to Dr. Gupta.

"I think he would have lived," Gupta said one year after the crash. "I don't know what his neurological status would've been. People always ask me, 'Would he have been able to play hockey?' No way, I can't tell you that. When he died of the infection, we were pretty confident he wouldn't die of his head injury at that point."

In the first few hours after her son died, LuAnn filled out paperwork. She also made sure to call family members before they got the bad news through the media. Just before midnight, she left the hospital with Jake, Erika, Michele Zarzaca and her husband Scott Cockerill, Don Waddell, Bob Hartley and Dan's girlfriend Lisa Rotondi. It occurred to LuAnn then that the physical connection she had always felt to Dan — the same feeling she felt when she arrived at Grady Hospital on the morning of the 30th — was gone. In one way, she could not help but be somewhat philosophical. She thought about the cyclical nature of life, how Dan was born at 8:30 in the morning and how he died at 8:30 at night.

Dan Snyder had always won the battles no one had expected him to win. That was why so many who knew him best expected him to pull through again. But this time, it was different. The battle was not winnable. As she left the hospital, LuAnn Snyder turned to her son Jake and uttered what all eight members of the "sad little entourage," as she called it, must have been thinking:

"I never thought we'd leave this hospital without him."

CHAPTER 5

A FUNERAL IN ELMIRA

Deb Good did not know who the large young men in suits were. They followed Dan Snyder's family from his home to the Elmira Mennonite Church for his memorial service and along the way, in a sign of kinship, they knuckle-punched, or "bumped," the children from Woolwich Township's minor hockey association who lined the streets. (Elmira's Sugar Kings have a rule that players cannot walk past a young fan without acknowledging him or her and giving a bump.) Deb Good would learn later that these men were NHL hockey players, members of the Atlanta Thrashers, and they were acknowledging what many who were present have called one of the most touching tributes made by the small town to its fallen hero.

Good had recently helped to organize a group of hockey

moms from the township's minor hockey association to help improve spirit and provide for more support for the township's programs. The group put on dances, tried to make the year-end banquet a bit fancier — what Good called "small community things." The news of Dan Snyder's death spread on Monday, October 6, and the service was to be held that Friday. With the following Monday being Canadian Thanksgiving, there was not much time to organize anything, but Good, in talking to her sister-in-law at the township's St. Jacobs arena, decided they ought to try and come up with some show of support for the Snyders.

She remains unsure of how they came up with the idea of having players from all of the township's programs line the streets wearing their jerseys and tapping their sticks in a silent show of respect. "We wanted to honour Danny somehow, and we came up with this idea," she said. "We had to fax these notices to the schools, because the kids had to come out of school. I thought I'd hear from the principals saying this is not appropriate. But I didn't have one call from one parent saying anything. The schools in the surrounding area thought it was a special tribute. There were no problems at all. Around noon, I think it was noon, we wanted all the kids to be there. There was a lot of coordinating. We met in the arena parking lot. I wanted to make sure the kids had refreshments. McDonald's donated things. I guess we thought it would be nice to do something. Everyone in town knows the Snyders. Graham is very involved in the Sugar Kings, and when one of your own makes the NHL, it's very special."

Good said she and the other mothers who volunteered were worried about the children's behaviour on such a solemn occasion. Out of the township's 1,000 children who were registered to play hockey, 350 showed up that day. Some were just small children whom she suspects did not understand the tragic event that had transpired. The older ones knew of Snyder and his achievements, the kind that placed this small corner of Canada on the grandest stage of a sport over which their community obsesses. Rather than misbehave, the children maintained their silent vigil and acted out the show of respect that hockey players almost always reserve for the ice. Then, spontaneously, they followed behind the funeral procession, walking towards the church until they were outside the steps.

Good said the idea was to let the Snyders know their family was special to the community.

"I don't know them," she said. "But in a small community when one of your own members of the community — and we're a pretty small one — makes it to the NHL, you're seen in the public eye, as well. Plus, they have a Mennonite background, like a lot of people in Elmira. That brings the community closer together. And they're involved in hockey their whole life. . . . All we think about — a lot of us think about — is hockey. It's a huge part of the community and everyone's life. . . . Graham is very involved in the hockey community. You'd see him around the rink a lot. That makes a big difference. And you know he's lost a son. If you make it to the Sugar Kings in this town, you're a hero. I have two boys. That's what I want my boys to do. It's huge when they make it."

People started arriving at the Elmira Mennonite Church 90 minutes before the service to get a seat. Before many of the guests arrived, Thrashers assistant public relations director

Rob Koch assisted Dany Heatley, who was on crutches after undergoing surgery three days earlier to repair his knee, to his seat. Heatley had to surrender his passport when charges were upgraded after Snyder's death to first-degree vehicular homicide, and needed special permission from the district attorney's office to attend the funeral.

The church's small, simple upstairs was completely occupied, as was the basement, filling the church to its capacity of 650. About 1,000 people were left outside. One of Snyder's agents, Don Reynolds, helped with logistics, such as making sure NHL commissioner Gary Bettman had a seat.

The Snyders' minister, Ruth Anne Laverty, began the service. "If you look at all the people who are here in this building and in Chateau Gardens and out on the lawn, indeed, it is a wonderful tribute to Dan and the Snyder family," she said. "I want to say welcome to all of you who have come from far away to attend this service. Shalom. May God's peace be with you. For a variety of reasons we have come to this memorial service. We're here to grieve — and we have some very deep tears. We're here to support each other. To celebrate the life of Dan. To wonder. To express that which we find difficult to put into words. With a variety of feelings we have come — feelings of pain, hurt, confusion, sorrow, to name a few."

The first speaker was Ray McKelvie, the man who drafted Snyder to play junior hockey with the Owen Sound Platers. McKelvie compared Snyder to a character in one of Canadian writer Scott Young's hockey novels, "an unbelievable story about a boy who had a dream — and a dream came true.

"Until I had met Dan, I had never met a young person who, unknowingly, had such a positive impact on so many young people," he said. "From day one in Owen Sound, Dan connected with fans, young hockey players, teachers and fellow players. Everywhere Dan went, he always seemed to be smiling and the centre of attention. A teacher at West Hill High School [the school from which Snyder graduated] once told me, 'If you want to find Dan, find a group of boys and girls enjoying themselves and laughing, and the boy in the middle smiling and enjoying himself the most will be Dan.' He led without knowing he was leading."

McKelvie told a story about a time late in Snyder's overage season when the team made a trade for defenceman Aaron Fransen. He worried he would have a hard time convincing Fransen to report. However, Fransen had attended the Maple Leafs rookie camp with Snyder that year, and did not need any convincing.

"Before I finished my spiel, he said, 'Mr. McKelvie, I'd be glad to come to Owen Sound and play with Dan Snyder.' That's a great tribute to Dan and that's the kind of leader he was.

"Twenty-five years is too short a lifetime," McKelvie concluded. "But we have some wonderful memories."

The next speaker was Rich Ennis, a friend of Graham's. Ennis is a sports psychologist who met Graham while working with Elmira's Junior B hockey team. Ennis was emotional, in part because he had initially turned down the Snyders' request to speak.

"It is with some guilt that I accept this distinct honour, because many here knew Dan better than I and many knew him for longer than I did," he said. "Originally, I used that as a reason to humbly decline this daunting task. After declining, however, I began reflecting on my nine-year friendship with Dan, and I realized that I did something Dan would never do: I'd been asked to set aside my personal concerns and feelings and make a contribution to a life of a friend and a family. Unlike Dan, I hesitated. So I stand before you apologetic, but determined to do what Dan would do — my best.

"If I could ask Dan how I could serve him today, I am certain of his answer. After reflecting for a moment, he would say, 'Maybe you could use some of that psychological junk of yours.'" A few laughs sprang from the pews. "'Use it to ease the pain of my friends and family.' Then he would smile . . . that mischievous little smile of his, because he would know he would have given me an impossible challenge. But I promise, like Dan, to do my best to please a friend.

"Let me begin by addressing Dan's friends. As one of you, let me offer this advice: resist the temptation to summarize what Dan's friendship meant to you, because it is not possible. It would be like trying to describe a great book in a few sentences. So much would be lost in the condensation. The true nature of your relationship with Dan lies in the daily details of the many moments you shared with him. I encourage you to look there for your friend. Recall the events that stand out in your memory. Elaborate on them. Complete the picture. Think of the time, the place, the occasion. See Dan. Hear Dan. That's where Dan lives — in the treasured memories that each of us hold. Instead of writing an epilogue to your friendship with Dan, revisit those chapters of your shared lives. And after each visit, ask yourself what those chapters meant. And what it told you about your friend."

Ennis related a story about Graham picking him up and taking him to one of Dan's games when Dan was Owen Sound's captain. Dan had a problem he wanted to discuss with Ennis. Speculating as to the nature of the problem, Ennis called Snyder "a sports psychologist's nightmare."

"I finally learned that Dan, as captain of Owen Sound, was frustrated by the lack of cohesion on the team. He was the captain and he wanted to change that, and he wanted my advice as to how to do that. As he described the difficulties, I wrote some suggestions on my napkin. Then I asked Dan what he had already done to improve the team dynamics. As he answered my question, I gradually scratched out all the ideas I had written down. Soon, everything on my napkin was eliminated. Then, Dan asked for my [advice]. As he had already exhausted all of my suggestions I planned on giving him, I resorted to the psychologist's best defence. I looked him squarely in the eyes and said, 'What do you think you should do?'

"It worked. Dan quickly laid out several other options he had been contemplating, and he outlined the advantages and disadvantages of each. We — and by we, I mean Dan — settled on a plan and he eventually put that plan into action. And as Ray already attested, such was the nature of his captaincy and his leadership. It's not a great event, merely an evening with Dan, but memories such as this will always keep me in touch with my friend Dan. And in that simple memory I see so much that I admired: I see Dan, my friend, Dan the selfless leader. Dan put the team ahead of himself. Hockey is a team game, and no player personified that more than Dan Snyder. When he accepted a role such as a captain, he embraced it, he accepted responsibility, he studied and learned whatever it took to be effective. I see Dan, my intelligent young friend, who knew how to tackle problems. And he found solutions. I see my friend Dan the determined achiever. Whenever he set his mind to achieving something, he turned it into reality."

Then Ennis addressed the family, his voice beginning to tremble. "I cannot fathom the pain you are suffering. I think of my own grief and imagine it multiplied 1,000-fold, and that still falls short. I cannot pretend to understand the nature and depth of your suffering. Perhaps I can offer you a different perspective on that pain.

"Emotions are arranged in opposite pairs. Joy and sadness go together. Emotions are also proportional. The greater you feel one emotion, the greater you will feel the opposite. Your intolerable sorrow is proportional to your insatiable love for Dan. The greater your joy in his life, the greater your sadness in his death. In the many dark days ahead, when it seems the grief is unbearable, remember the source of your anger: the joy. Remember the 25 years of loving Dan and being loved by Dan. LuAnn, you said you were blessed with the opportunity to love such a wonderful son. I hope you and your family cling tenaciously to that truth. Your suffering is a testament to that joyous blessing."

Dan's uncle Jeff spoke next. Jeff had coached Dan in Elmira, then coached against him in the OHL when Jeff became coach of the Kitchener Rangers while Dan was playing in Owen Sound, creating quite a dilemma for Dan's grandparents as to which team to cheer for at those games. His voice catching at times, Jeff Snyder spoke of a side of Dan his friends in Atlanta often mentioned, about how Dan was so proud of his family.

"As a friend, Dan was very inspirational. As he climbed the hockey ladder to reach its highest level, he never changed. He was the same Dan he had always been. He remained humble, and stayed close to his family and friends back home. Dan was very generous, always giving time to help other people, and he was a great role model for kids. Our family was very proud of his work with different charities in the communities he played in. I was especially proud of the work he did with the Kidney Foundation.

"I will always cherish the night this past June, when Dan called and asked if I wanted to watch a playoff hockey game on TV that night. He spent time with my two daughters. We sat down in my rec room, just the two of us. We talked about how far his game had come, and the excitement of becoming a solid NHL player. We shared a few brown pops and shared stories. It was a great night that I will treasure forever. I hope you know how very proud I am of you. You touched so many lives in such a short time. I will continue to miss you, and you will continue to inspire me to be the best person I can be. I miss you very much."

During his teenage years, Jake Snyder had the kind of relationship with his brother Dan, who was three and a half years younger, that made bickering and fighting a constant. Whether it was street hockey or video games, the brothers were competitive, and Jake often fell victim to his brother's notoriously sharp tongue, leading to the kind of altercations for which brothers are famous.

"I guess he always had a way of pushing the right buttons and getting people pissed off," Jake said. "I've always been really competitive. It didn't take much to set me off. He enjoyed it a little bit. He'd usually end up taking a pretty good thumping."

In addition to their competitive instincts, both boys inherited a passion for hockey from their father. Jake's talents as a goaltender never got him past the junior level. He would occasionally get called up to the Sugar Kings, and his claim to fame came in a game in which he appeared opposite Marty Turco, now one of the NHL's best goalies, playing with the Dallas Stars. At 30, Jake quenches his thirst for hockey by coaching, and by playing on so many teams during the winter that at times it seems he's at the rink every night of the week.

While his love for his country's national sport did not make him unique, one thing did — he had a brother who made it to the National Hockey League. Growing up in Elmira, Jake and Dan shared the dreams of all sports-minded boys who one day hoped to be professionals. As Dan's career in minor hockey progressed, Jake was one of his champions. He attended virtually all his brother's home games during his junior career, 90 minutes away in Owen Sound. Jake had a hunch that bigger things were coming.

"By his third year, when he was the captain, I thought he was definitely going to move on and keep working his way up," Jake said. "He was able to prove a lot of people wrong. I didn't see any of the knocks. People said he was too small, maybe not quite offensive enough, which I never agreed with." When Dan moved on to the Chicago Wolves, Jake made as many playoff games as possible, despite the seven-hour drive.

As the brothers left boyhood behind and became men, the bickering faded, a vestigial by-product of youth. The relationship solidified and they talked about things like standing up for each other at their respective weddings. After Dan died, much was made of the closeness between the two brothers. That left some to wonder what Jake's reception might be to Dany Heatley. To this point, the Snyders had very publicly supported Heatley. Might there be a schism? Such were the questions and the task before Jake in giving his brother's eulogy.

"I think it was definitely helpful to write a lot of those things down," Jake said of writing the eulogy. "Even in the time he was in the hospital, you're there and you have a lot of time to think. It brought back a lot of memories I hadn't had time to think about — not that I was preparing for that, but it was the outcome. I was thinking about the memories. When I got home, it was something I felt I needed to do. I knew some people who were attending didn't know Dan that well, and I thought that they should. It was definitely difficult writing those things down. I had a tougher time getting those things down than I did saying them. I didn't finish until 4:30 a.m. At the memorial service, I was nervous and shaking when I was in the church. It was just a really strange feeling. Not like he was there with you, but I thought, 'You can help me get through this' and I just felt fine."

Jake stepped to the pulpit obviously emotional, but also with a bit of a bounce and a sense of wit. His pride in his brother was clear — but so were the good-natured remnants of sibling rivalry. "I've heard people in a lot of the tributes over the last few days speak about Dan's leadership skills, and that he was a born leader," Jake said. "He was definitely a leader. But I'd question whether he was born that way." Laughter filled the church. "I think it took a little bit to develop these skills, but it was really nice for me to be able to be a part of that and watch him grow into the person he became."

Jake recounted stories from the family's old house — playing hockey in the basement on the carpet where the brothers painted blue lines and a centre red line — where he would make five-year-old Dan stand while he sang "O, Canada" before each game. He talked about how Dan's first media interview was probably with Jake posing as Dave Hodge, then one of the hosts of *Hockey Night in Canada*.

In recounting Dan's ability to torment him through competition, Jake expressed sympathy for his brother's opponents on the ice. "I got a lot of enjoyment out of watching him commence his pro hockey career, and watching guys chase him around the ice and thinking, 'Buddy, I know exactly what you're thinking right now,'" he said. He reiterated his brother's pride in his hometown and how whenever teams would try to list it as Kitchener, the closest big city, Dan would say, "I'm not from Kitchener, I'm from Elmira, and that's how you're going to put that."

Then Jake addressed his brother's former teammates in Chicago and Atlanta. As his father had done in addressing the Thrashers before their first exhibition game after the accident, Jake picked up on the theme of using Dan as an inspiration. "When things get tough in the weeks and months to come, I want you to use my brother as an example of how you persevere, and how he overcame obstacles. And above all, you go out there and play with heart every night. When you need a laugh, you think of something my brother did off the ice, because every story about my brother ends in a good laugh. Dan's always been an integral part of this organization. Please make sure he's a part of yours this year. And in years to come."

Then Jake spoke directly to Dany Heatley, looking squarely at Dan's friend, who sat towards the front of the church to Jake's right. "To Dany, one thing that always happened whenever I visited my brother, whether it be in Orlando or Chicago, all of his teammates treated me as a friend, as one of the guys, any time we would go out. That's the way they were. If you were to come here to Elmira, the same thing would always happen here. My friends are your friends. I know from talking to my brother often, that you two had become really good friends and shared a lot of great experiences together. If you're one of Dan's guys, you're one of my guys. Friends look out for each other, no matter how tough the circumstances. So I will look out for you as much as I can, because I know that is exactly what my brother would want."

Finally, in a heartfelt soliloquy, he spoke to his brother. "And Dan, young Daniel — you know, I think I would've called you that if we were both in our 90s — you'll always be young Daniel to me; I called you that all the time. I hope you realize how much I already miss you as a friend, and how much everybody misses you as a teammate and a son. My sister and I really miss our brother right now. I really wish I could talk to you right now. I can talk to you right now, I just wish I could hear back from you. All those stories and all that joy you brought to me, I'm going to carry that in my heart with me for the rest of my life. I thought many a time, when you made it to the NHL, I might have talked about you a little bit too much, to my friends and stuff like that. To me, it never made me feel more important because my brother was playing in the NHL. I just did it because I was so very proud of you.

"You know, anyone who thought I talked about you too much before better get used to me talking about you more now, because I think the whole world is starting to realize what a person Dan really was. I had occasion to talk to a good friend of Dan's, Jarrod Skalde, the other night, and this is after Dan had passed away. And Jarrod said, 'You know Jake, you don't run across guys like Dan in hockey every day.' And I said, 'You know what Jarrod? You don't run into people like Dan Snyder in your *life* every day.' Dan Snyder the hockey player is nothing compared to Dan Snyder the man, Dan Snyder the friend, Dan Snyder the brother, Dan Snyder the son. I promised you the last time that I saw you that I would remind people how you battled right to the last moment of your life. You were the toughest person I've ever known. You spent our childhood years trying to be just like me, and I will do my absolute best for the rest of my life to be just like you. Dan, you are, and you always will be, my best friend. I will think about you always and I will always love you."

When Jake concluded, he walked back to his seat, where he was embraced by his father. The next speaker was Todd Reynolds, Dan's agent. Reynolds' father, Don, is a longtime agent and Todd joined the small family business. A goalie at Boston's Northeastern University, Todd Reynolds handled negotiations for Dan and the pair were close in age, only six years apart. Reynolds had trouble composing himself as he prepared to read a letter written to Snyder by an Owen Sound Platers' season-ticket holder named Paul Alisauskas, shortly after Snyder's junior career ended. The letter read, in part: "Since you've played your last game as a Plater, I thought I'd share a few of my thoughts on your tenure with the team. I've never written to anyone like this before, but felt your departure shouldn't pass without comment, because of all the enjoyment you've given the fans and, perhaps more importantly, the way you've conducted yourself throughout.

"I remember your first year here. Several of us armchair coaches had our doubts about whether that scrawny kid would make the team. Nevertheless, one thing we were *never* in doubt about was that you'd die *trying*. That sort of set the tone for the rest of your stay here.

"I guess your first year had a 'prove yourself' quality to it.

You left me (and many others) shaking our heads at some of the goons you refused to back down from. As you clawed your way into the lineup, all of us realized that, whatever skill level you may or may not have, this was one player who *never* left anything in the tank. . . .

"Your leadership and maturity as a captain was inspiring to us fans and, much more importantly, to your team. Any time you were out of the lineup; it just wasn't the same team. I know how difficult it was for you to take the abuse and punishment which came your way over the last two years, and to skate away without retaliating. However, you led by example and made almost every Plater better for it. . . .

"The Platers have had some fine captains during their time in Owen Sound. Having seen them all, I have no reservations whatsoever about saying you were the finest I've seen. You've given both on and off the ice with class, dignity and selflessness.

"You and I have never formally met. However, I remember I once asked you to sign a jersey for my neighbour's son, your biggest fan. The time you took with him and the way you spoke to him left him beaming for a week. I'll never forget you for that.

"I don't know what your future will bring. If professional hockey is what you want out of life, they'll have to call in the military if they want to keep you out of it. Whatever happens, I know I've seen a young man who will be a great success in life, wherever he goes. Please take with you our hopes and prayers for that bright and prosperous future. You've given us all a lot to remember you by."

The Thrashers opened their season on Thursday, October 9, just four days after Snyder's death. They were scheduled to play the Columbus Blue Jackets at Philips Arena, fly to Elmira after the game to attend Snyder's funeral on Friday, then fly directly afterwards to Washington for their first road game — a daunting schedule to say the least. Before the game against Columbus, the Thrashers held a pre-game ceremony to honour Snyder. Bagpipers solemnly intoned "Amazing Grace." The scoreboard played a highlight reel of Snyder's career ending with, "Dan Snyder, 1978–2003," and the sold-out arena paused for a moment of silence.

To say that winning the game was important to the team was an understatement. No one knew what to expect of the Thrashers, even playing against a team that was likely to dwell at the bottom of the league's standings again. With less than three minutes remaining, the teams were locked in a 1–1 tie. Then, the most unlikely of heroes — defenceman Chris Tamer, who had just one goal in 72 games the previous season — stepped into a slapshot from just inside the blue line and beat Blue Jackets goalie Marc Denis for the game winner with 2:24 left in regulation. Afterwards, in the dressing room, TurnerSouth cameras captured coach Bob Hartley flipping the game-winning puck to Snyder's good friend Joey Guilmet, the assistant equipment manager. Guilmet would present the puck to the Snyders on the day of the funeral. LuAnn Snyder keeps the precious token in a dresser drawer in her bedroom.

When the speakers for Dan's memorial service were chosen, LuAnn made a special call to Hartley, whom her son had adored. "It just wouldn't have been right without him," she said. Don Lismer, from Hockey Ministries International, spoke after Reynolds and Lismer was followed by Dale

Bauman, who had served as the Snyder's minister when their children were young. Ruth Anne Laverty, the minister presiding over the service, began making announcements to conclude the service, when Bauman walked up and whispered something to her.

"I just heard that Dan's coach from Atlanta is supposed to speak," she interrupted herself. "Would he come forward?"

Hartley bounded up to the pulpit, and quipped in his clipped French-Canadian accent, "I thought I would have to call a timeout." He thanked the Snyders for their strength and for the seeming paradox of how they supported the Thrashers organization at a time when they should have been the ones receiving support. He began with a light touch:

"And last night, thank you to my players for getting that famous game puck for the Snyder family," he said. "And also, thank you to those hundreds of young players in the streets. They reminded me of good old Snydes — banging their sticks everywhere while being respectful. That's good old Snydes. I could see some of those young kids missing teeth, hair all over the place, just like Snydes would show up at practice in the morning."

Hartley told a story about the first time he met Snyder on January 21 earlier that year, when the Thrashers were set to play the playoff-contending St. Louis Blues. Hartley had been on the job for one week, and the Thrashers were well out of the playoff picture while the Blues were looking at one of the top spots in the Western Conference. Hartley told general manager Don Waddell that he wanted to get a look at the team's prospects, players who would build the team's future. Snyder arrived for the Blues game without benefit of a practice. "So I asked Steve Weeks, my lone partner at the time,

'Who is that Snyder boy?' He said, 'Oh, you'll love him. He's your type of player.' So I said, 'Go and get him and I'll show him a little video of how we play.' And here comes that kid. I couldn't believe what I was seeing. Here comes this kid who has the legs the size of a broomstick. And I was saying, 'This kid is going to play an NHL game?'

"And we're playing the St. Louis Blues and we're playing a great game. We're leading 2–0 and it's maybe 13 minutes left in the first period, and here's Snydes on the ice and we had talked about being disciplined, especially against a great team like St. Louis. And right in front of our bench, he elbows one of the Blues. He was always a great listener." Some chuckles spread through the church. "So after the first period I told Weeksy, 'Go and get that Snyder.' So I'm in my office and I pointed in his stomach and I said, 'Listen to me, young man. You know what?' I said, 'Chicago will get closer to Atlanta if ever you do this again.' I said, 'I'm aware of all the flights from Chicago to Atlanta. You take one more stupid penalty and you're gone.'

"And you know what? He went back and played a great second and third period. The next morning he's in my office, telling me that he didn't want to go back to Chicago. That was . . ." Hartley's mood changed swiftly from jovial to over-whelmed. He stopped in mid-sentence for nearly 20 seconds. He rubbed the side of his face with his right hand, trembling. He looked up and breathed heavily before resuming: "That was Snydes. I'm sorry. That was big Snydes."

He continued with another story. "A couple of weeks later, I'm going to play my former team in Colorado, and we're in Vancouver two nights before and I don't even want to say the score. It's a touchdown plus another couple of points. We get beat. We get slapped. So we're in Colorado the next day, practising. We start to prepare a couple of guys for definitely my biggest game of the season, and Snydes walks up to me after practice — and I never said a word to no one — he said, 'We're going to win it. Whatever I need to do, just ask me.' So Snydes, he became one of my favourite boys. One of the boys I knew whether on the road or at home, 1–1 game, 5–1 game, he'd be there.

"So I gave him an easy job — to be the cover man for Peter Forsberg. That was the morning of the game. He came back after the pre-game meal, came back to the rink and he said, 'Can I ask you a question?' 'Sure.' 'I'll cover Forsberg and he won't do much, but can I play one shift versus Joe Sakic? He's my idol.' And, again, that was Snydes. He wanted to do his job, and he always wanted to measure himself against the best — always beating the odds. Never bet against Snydes, because you're going to lose. . . .

"Throughout the summer I talked to Snydes maybe two or three times, and he was telling me how he was so excited about this season. What a great kid. What a great kid. Even during training camp, he was on rehab. Every day I would check with the medical staff and I would get one news: he was already ahead of his rehab. He would be skating by now. Again, beating the odds, that was his specialty. Making people look like fools. That was Snydes with that little, little smirk."

He ended on a philosophical note. "On behalf of coaches and management, your fellow players, 25 years is way too early to leave the Thrashers' nest. But I really believe he left the nest to fly above us to keep his eyes on us. And if I can talk like a coach for a minute, the best way to remember Snydes would be to transform this great church for a minute into a hockey rink. And make sure that we all leave the way Snydes would leave the rink after a big win and a job well done, because that was big Snydes. Make sure you leave this church with a smile. Be proud of him. Because he's proud of us."

Ruth Anne Laverty dismissed the congregation with a benediction: "Go in love, for love alone endures. Go in peace for it is the gift of God. Go in safety for we cannot go where God is not."

CHAPTER 6

THE FOUNTAIN OF MEMORIES AND THE ROAD TO HEALING

It was getting to the point, Gerlinde Petz said, that the teen-agers of Elmira were starting to feel as if their town was cursed.

Adam Leigh Schmidt. Michael J. Jongerius. Kevin Cronin. Andrew Wagner. Rafal Gidzinski. Jeff Clemmer. Colin Melitzer. Rob Olsen. Zachary Johnston. Michael MacKenzie.

In the years 2000 and 2001, these 10 — all boys or young men — died, most in automobile accidents. The first to die, on March 10, 2000, was 18-year-old Andrew Wagner, a passenger in a car that was hit from behind. In two years, there were eight separate fatal motor vehicle accidents in all. Six of the eight accidents were single fatalities; the other two both claimed two lives. But there were also others who, while surviving, suffered serious injuries that disabled them for the rest of their lives. Most of the accidents were local to Woolwich

Township, but one, involving Adam Schmidt, occurred in Kelowna, British Columbia. Five of the accidents came during one horrifying stretch from August to October 2000, totaling seven deaths. The toll that grief took on the young people of the township of 18,000 was palpable.

Petz, who works at Woolwich Interfaith, a counselling centre set up in 1976, and her friend Linda Bell, the pastor of Gale Presbyterian in Elmira, decided something needed to be done.

"Our community is really a very tightly knit one, in the sense that when something like this happens everyone is touched by it," Petz said. "It's not like a larger community, where you might just hear about it. People know someone affected by it in Elmira. I'm a counsellor. We would see a lot of people from the community. They'd be seeking counselling for something, but this issue about the loss of the children, the youth, always came up. There was this fog over Elmira. The kids themselves were starting to be afraid there was a curse. I heard that word."

As the community examined ways of trying to address the problem, Petz and Bell searched for something that might lead to some sense of healing. "We were having lunch and we thought we really, really need to do something," Petz said.

Bell explained what she liked about the idea of a fountain. "For me — and in most of the world — water is the symbol of life and rebirth, and of hope," she said. "For me, the idea of the water and the sunlight dancing together, it's a very theological premise."

They found a sympathetic ear in Larry Devitt, a friend who runs the township's parks and recreation department. Devitt helped the women to make a presentation to the town's council. The project gained momentum.

"Linda and I at least were very clear that we wanted something right in the middle of town," Petz said. "Kids were most affected. The high school is nearby, and we wanted it to be something they would be passing every day. So these [deceased] kids would be part of the texture of the community." For his part, Devitt described the community as "reeling."

"It seemed that you'd hardly get a chance to catch your breath and there was another accident," he said. "It was just being hammered continually. I don't know how else to describe it. We have a neighbour who lost a son. So you feel the pain. I knew a lot of these kids. I can't describe how the families felt. It just kept coming back and coming back."

Within months, townspeople had donated $95,000. The town had set a goal of about $45,000, and Bell said organizers made every effort to let people know they were reaching their goal, but the money kept pouring in. Jim Schwindt, an engineer and member of Bell's congregation, was instrumental in donating his time, telling Bell "it was an honour and a privilege." In the end, the project took in nearly twice its goal in donations. The remaining $45,000 was turned back into the park system to help fund other projects. The result, dedicated on August 19, 2001, is what the people of Elmira call "The Fountain of Memories." The day the monument was dedicated, the town closed the streets and more than 1,000 people attended the ceremony, despite intermittent rain. A high school choir group sang. At the appointed moment, water sprang forth from the fountain. "It was an awesome day," Bell said.

Just a short walk down Park Avenue from Graham and LuAnn's home is the intersection of Hampton and Arthur Streets in the centre of Elmira. Three large, black marble tablets sit at angles facing each other, flanking the fountain that sits in their centre. Fifty-five names in total are engraved on the tablets. The township has only two criteria for listing young people's names on the monument: they must have been under 25 at the time of death, and have lived in the township or attended Elmira District Secondary School, which draws some students from outside Woolwich's borders. The township does not add names to the monument unless the parents of the deceased make the request. The town also did not place any date restrictions on the date of death. For a community that has suffered so much, the decision was made in the knowledge that all deaths, no matter how far back in time, were equal. Who was to say that a child who died four decades ago was missed any less than one who died a few months ago? Or one that was hardly known to its own parents?

"[The monument] doesn't deny the pain, but it also talks about hope," Bell said. "And very much recognizes these 10 young men, but also others. We've got a couple of stillborns whose names are there. Whether they had just been in this world a moment or 25 years, they impact the lives of [someone] in the community and, therefore, the [whole] community. We widened it to any kind of death. Someone said, 'What if it's a suicide?' We decided to include anyone, regardless of cause. It wasn't a prolonged discussion." The earliest memorialized death was in 1959.

Each year, as summer fades and fall is set to begin, the township adds new names. In 2004, two names were added: Keri Versteeg (1989–2003) and Dan Snyder (1978–2003).

Graham Snyder stood uneasily on the ice, holding a microphone in one hand and some rumpled handwritten notes in the other. He spoke cautiously and slowly, as though walking over a frozen pond he was not quite sure was safe. His voice quavered, perhaps from nerves, perhaps from emotions.

"I'd rather not be here," he said. "I know how hard it is to lose a brother or a son." He was in a rink in the small farming community of Blenheim, not far from LuAnn's hometown of Chatham. His audience was young hockey players and their families, packed to the rink's capacity of about 2,000.

Public speaking is not something that comes easily to him, but Graham has forced himself to do it, believing it will help him through the grieving process in his son's death. On that cold day in December 2004, he shared his grief with another family. The Snyders were invited to speak at the skills competition of the 32nd Golden Acres/Susan Rumble Memorial Tournament. The previous year, the skills competition was won by 12-year-old Weston De Brouwer, who was later killed in an accident involving an off-road vehicle. On the drive to the rink, LuAnn mentioned that Weston De Brouwer, whose nickname was "Cowboy," "sounds a lot like Dan."

Graham's speech continued. "The way he's been described to me, Weston was a very special young man. He knew the importance of team, of teamwork. [The skills competition] was fun for me, it brings back memories. Skills are very important in the game of hockey. Other skills don't show up as easily. Weston had them, and they also served my son Dan well. Dan was just like the guy who wiped out earlier on the first turn, and had to get up and catch up. He was never the fastest skater or the best goal-scorer. But one important thing he learned early on was the importance of teamwork and contributing to the team. It's not always possible to be the top scorer, but there is a role for all of us. It might be checking another player who is a big scorer. Or making a big check. Or getting in somebody's way — doing whatever it takes. That's what my son loved to do — those things — however he could make the team do better. Cowboy wasn't the best goal-scorer, but he would do anything to help his team in any way."

One would never mistake Graham for an orator, but the audience was rapt and the banal setting was transformed into something solemn. Graham also sensed something in the audience that day, and altered his message from one of teamwork to a topic that transcended hockey. He departed from his notes and elected to speak more about life.

"As we gather here to honour Weston, it's important to talk about support from friends, families and community — the support of the hockey community," he said clumsily, dropping his notes, then interrupting himself to lean over and pick them up. "Not only our own children, but others, are a big part of our lives. Enjoying the game is a big part of what will help you. It's something you can help your teammates do. In a number of cases, Dan's teammates told me that they liked to sit and talk with him about how much fun they were having.

"In closing, it's very hard to lose someone we love who is close to us. One of the things we can help each other to do is to treasure the gifts left for us by Cowboy. When you're out there playing the game, if you're not having fun, think about him — how much he loved the game, how much he gave to it. That's what we're here for — to enjoy the game — wherever it may take us."

Then, in another improvised moment, Graham brought some in the crowd to tears. "At Dan's funeral, they lined the town and stood in a very touching show of respect. I would like to ask the players on the ice to tap their sticks in [De Brouwer's] honour. People in the stands, please take a minute to stand, and [players] quietly tap your sticks on the ice." The rhythmic sound of children clattering their sticks on the ice softly reverberated through the silence of the rink.

Ben De Brouwer, a tall, sturdy man summoning the strength he needed for this moment, stepped up to the microphone. He headed a small contingent of family members wearing cowboy hats in homage to Weston. Ben De Brouwer barely stammered out a few words. "It's funny how someone from so far away, who didn't even know him, can hit the nail on the head," De Brouwer said of Graham's speech. "There was no one who worked harder than Cowboy." Then, with the audience still in reverential silence, his wife, Patricia, thanked the community for its support during what she called a very hard time.

Later, LuAnn Snyder would comment on her own inability to speak publicly about Dan — which lies in contrast to the public speaking she does professionally in her role as a volunteer firefighter, talking to children about fire safety. "To stand there and talk about Dan, it would be too hard for me to do," she said. "It's too emotional. I just know I couldn't get through it."

After the speeches, Graham and LuAnn waited to meet the De Brouwers. The setting was as familiar as any to LuAnn. "Saturday at the rink," she said, squeezing past the throng headed for the concession stand, where they could purchase a greasy mystery meat product happily christened "breakfast on a bun." When the Snyders and De Brouwers met in the rink's cramped lobby — standing just feet from a framed photo of Weston housed inside a trophy case — it was as if they had known each other for years despite the physical distance they lived from each other and the 10-years difference in age. Perhaps it was because they shared each other's grief. The two families are part of an exclusive club in which neither they nor anyone else wants membership.

For more than half an hour they simply talked about their children. "Their boy, our boy," Graham said. "There were a lot of similarities." "A carbon copy," chimed in LuAnn. "It sounded like the same kid." They traded phone numbers before the Snyders departed.

In the car on the ride back to Elmira, Graham spoke about why he accepts requests like the Blenheim tournament, in spite of his obvious discomfort. "It's certainly a little different for me. Sometimes I feel comfortable doing it, other times I don't. Today, I didn't feel real comfortable. It's a little hard standing out on the ice. One of the things I find, for me, is that it's somewhat therapeutic. It forces me to put some of my thoughts down on paper in an order or a sequence and analyze them a little bit. From that standpoint, it's helpful to me." Nonetheless, Graham said he does not force himself to do it. "I wouldn't say that. I probably wouldn't have been doing it two years ago. I've never really done much speaking at all."

In the weeks following Dan's death, Graham and Jake did interviews with several major Canadian media outlets. Facing the camera is one kind of anxiety, facing an audience is another. Graham was first asked to speak at Elmira's minor hockey banquet in the spring of 2004. "That is kind of a different thing," he said in comparing it to television. "When I did the first one, I wasn't comfortable at all. I didn't feel it came across real well, but the people are very forgiving," he said with a laugh. Nonetheless, LuAnn said people were grateful that her husband spoke and were generous in their assessments. Graham did not feel much better about the Blenheim talk. "To be honest, I didn't feel real good about the way it went today, but I knew people were so glad that we had come that it didn't matter that I didn't have the right words to say."

Graham said asking the players to make the gesture of tapping their sticks occurred to him spontaneously. "That was something that was very, very touching at Dan's funeral." LuAnn agreed. "When we came around the corner of the house — that's a long stretch — the whole stretch was lined. Boys and girls, tapping their sticks. The Thrashers [players] had talked about how much it meant for these kids to see the NHL players, to high-five some of these kids, and a lot of the guys did. [The players] were very, very moved. They had never seen anything like it." Graham continued, "I think some of the players were almost mystified by it. They found it hard to fathom, especially the ones who weren't Canadian. [Thrashers captain] Shawn McEachern told me that."

"They were so amazed," LuAnn added. "A small community like that, Dan was a part of everybody there. He always had a connection. Somebody knew somebody from his family or his uncle. 'Well, I worked with his mother.' Everybody knew somebody. It gives you a sense of familiarity that you knew that person, but it's part of your community and you belong to that. I think that's why so many people took it so hard."

As they returned to Elmira, LuAnn reflected upon the emotions the De Brouwers were experiencing, as well as the unfortunate group in which she and Graham were members.

"People send us letters and they start off saying, 'You don't know us, but we lost a child or a daughter, and we saw what happened to you in the paper . . .' Total and complete strangers. At the beginning, you're so numb. You're in a bit of a daze. Sometimes you hardly remember [the first few months]. [Ben De Brouwer] was such a nice man, easygoing. It was all he could do to get those few words out."

In the weeks before his speech in Blenheim, Graham also spoke in a more intimate setting. To help deal with the inordinate number of tragic deaths to its young people, local churches in the Elmira area began "services of healing and hope." There, surviving family members met in an informal setting to try to come to grips with their feelings of loss, and achieve some kind of healing and closure. During the first year of these services about 450 people attended.

The Snyders' minister, Ruth Anne Laverty, believes that the community of Elmira works to comfort its own in a time of need, in part, because so many have shared in the grief. "There's a sense of working together that's important in this community," said Laverty, who was not born in Elmira. "There are 13 churches [from the surrounding area] that make up an ecumenical council. The Maple Syrup Festival is a big part of our community. There's a sense of working together. When Dan died, I started getting calls saying, 'Is there a way we can help?' Another church gave us 350 chairs for the funeral. 'If you need any help, we'll help.' We couldn't have done it by ourselves. It was the largest funeral the church has ever had."

Besides the Syrup Festival, there are other ways the small

community comes together. Laverty said each winter there is a "toques, hats and scarves campaign." Another example was the contribution the minor hockey association made at Dan's funeral. People volunteered to make the procession memorable and touching.

"When tragedies happen, the community comes together," Laverty said. "I think it does [help]. The strength of the community walks with each other. . . . You can feel lifted up by other people praying and supporting us so that we we're not all left alone by ourselves."

The services of healing and hope were scheduled to take place before the Christmas holiday in early December, to help families cope with the loss of loved ones at that difficult time. "These are hard times for families at the table," Laverty said. "It's even different from public speaking. It's a valuable place to talk about your pain. We talk about getting closure on our process of healing, and coming to accept the loss. When we least expect it, there's another little place where there's pain. We journey with our grief. We journey with pain and gradually let go."

The services, held twice before the holiday season, are called "A Time to Remember." The township's interfaith council chooses the program each year. During the ceremony, there are four speakers, and each lights a candle. The night Graham Snyder spoke, the topics included past Christmases with Dan, and what it would be like in the future.

"Graham spoke of how forgiveness is part of grief," said Petz, also one of the speakers. "In order to resolve the grief, you have to forgive. All the people who were there — and there were 150 at each — each one will go up. They get a candle and they light it in memory of someone they've lost.

It's a very beautiful ceremony."

Linda Bell is a devoted fan of the Kitchener Rangers and knew Graham's brother Jeff was the team's one-time coach. She had also attended a clinic where LuAnn worked as a nurse. "He is a remarkable man, they're remarkable parents," Bell said of Graham and LuAnn. "The amount they give to the community. The heart they have for the people they work with. They do, they give a great deal, mostly in the area of sports, but this is very much a hockey community."

Gerlinde Petz came to work at Woolwich Interfaith in 1996. Its mission is to provide counselling guided by spirituality. Petz says the council was founded at a time when many people were moving away from that kind of spirituality. "It was started in 1976 by a bunch of people in Elmira who thought it deserved its own counselling centre instead of having to go to the big cities of Kitchener and Waterloo," she said. "It's not a Christian agency, but spirituality needs to be one of the things that is an option to be discussed. In the '70s and before, there was this attitude and approach that 'it's all about the reason, and so forth.' The interfaith movement said that religion is an integral part of people's lives. In grieving situations, it's absolutely essential. We've certainly grown a lot. At the time when I started, we were seeing perhaps 300 people in a year. Now we're seeing more like a thousand. It's every kind of counselling: individuals, couples, family, group. Whatever the issues people bring. Grief, breakdowns in relationships."

Coping with death is difficult enough for adults. For young adults — so often imbued with a sense of invincibility — it can be a shattering experience. This has been the challenge for many of the teachers and administrators at Elmira District Secondary School.

"The teachers and the principals, they've been so good at addressing it," Petz said. "There hasn't been an attempt to put it underneath, to bury it." Petz described how the school reacted in fall 2004, after another accidental death of one of its students, a boy who fell from a farm silo. "Our agency actually has a counsellor at E.D.S.S. three days a week," she said. "There are issues. You need someone there three days a week because the issues are too big to deal with. There were 20 kids who were just devastated. In December, and even now, this group is quite big. A grief group. Yet another teenage boy who died. I don't think the distinction is made, 'Well, this is a different kind of act [from a motor vehicle accident].' It happened, and he died way before his time. What have we lost in potential, not to mention who he was right now?"

What makes Elmira's pain so sharp is its seemingly unbroken succession over time. Before the series of deaths starting in March 2000, the town experienced a first spasm of grief. Known colloquially as "the Wideman accident," four teenage boys were killed in 1984 when a hay ride they were on was hit by a car. The search for meaning can often be bewildering, especially for teenagers trying to cope with the loss of people their own age.

"Personally, I don't try to explain this," Petz said. "What I try to do is really address the grief or the sadness that anybody's death, especially a young person's death, means. If you address those feelings, you can get to the point where you find the strength to reinvest in life. I don't say, 'Oh, it's God's will,' because I think that's a bromide. I don't believe in that. Why would it happen? They need to look at that. What are all of the reasons they can look at? I don't think there is a reason. In some cases, people tried to say it was the drinking. Most kids had not been drinking. That's not an explanation. It was more about addressing the fears about having the curse descending. It was a dark cloud in the township. With the fountain of memories, you could externalize that and make it something. It changed how people viewed the sequence, the series of events. . . . It really is a very moving memorial, so [the town's teenagers] can be with them. The names are there. I've heard kids say it's like they're there. It's a reinvestment in life. It changes how we could look at those deaths, because we were all a community trying to find meaning."

Yet even the healing the fountain hoped to provide could only be temporary. It was dedicated on August 19, 2001, but before the year ended another young Elmiran had died. About two years later, Dan Snyder's death reopened those wounds. "I recall somebody saying with a great deal of apprehension, 'Oh, my God, it's not going to happen again,'" Petz said. "The people who were around, there was this sense of fear. Dan Snyder was a great hero to people in Elmira, so it made it a stronger fear. It was coupled with so much sadness."

It seems one small town has suffered almost beyond what it can bear. "I think that's what makes it so pivotal when people say, 'What's the meaning of this?'" Petz said. "Because it is disproportionate. The town of Elmira has 7,000 people. The question people ask of me, 'It's almost like we're in the Bermuda Triangle. Why?' There's no reason, no explanation for that. That one's a lot harder to answer."

CHAPTER 7

"NOTHING LOVED
IS EVER LOST"

The Thrashers left Elmira after Dan Snyder's memorial service and flew directly to Washington for their first road game the next day. The charter plane dropped off players, coaches and the general manager, and returned to Atlanta with some corporate officers, team staff and Dany Heatley. In that game after the memorial service, the Thrashers defeated the Capitals 4-3, to start the season 2–0 for the first time in team history. It also was the first time they had ever beaten Washington on the road. Journeyman Randy Robitaille, who had just joined the organization that summer, talked of what the team had gone through after scoring a goal and recording two assists in the win.

"Obviously, it's been tough the last few weeks," Robitaille said. "But the team has been doing a great job of battling through at game time. It's taking our mind off it and using it as motivation. [Dany Heatley and Dan Snyder] are both in our hearts, and we're trying to play some good hockey and not think about it."

Then came two ties: 2–2 at home against the New York Islanders, and 0–0 against the New York Rangers in Madison Square Garden. Next, the Thrashers came home and pummeled the Chicago Blackhawks 7–2, as Ilya Kovalchuk recorded a hat trick, giving him five goals in the first five games. The Thrashers' first defeat came on October 21 at Tampa Bay, against the eventual Stanley Cup champion. But it was no garden variety loss, and it did not stop the Thrashers' point streak. Down 2–0 with less than four minutes remaining in regulation, Kovalchuk and Marc Savard scored less than two minutes apart to send the game into overtime. Tampa Bay's Pavel Kubina won the game with a fluky shorthanded goal, 3–2, but the Thrashers had points in their first six games and were 3–0–2–1.

The Lightning game started a trend in which the Thrashers showed an uncanny ability to rally after getting behind in the score. The next game, they fell down 2–0 again at home against Nashville, but Kovalchuk erupted for another hat trick in the eventual 4–2 win. He now had nine goals in his past six games. The next game, against Florida, Kovalchuk scored again but the Thrashers lost for the first time in regulation on October 25, 3–2.

They got back in the win column on October 27 at Toronto, a 3–2 overtime victory. Down 2–0 at the Air Canada Centre with less than eight minutes remaining in regulation, Savard and winger Jeff Cowan scored 22 seconds apart to tie the game. Then in overtime, after killing off four minutes of a 3-on-2, after Andy Sutton was called for elbowing and unsportsmanlike conduct, Savard scored with 15 seconds remaining with

Kovalchuk assisting. The Thrashers were 5–1– 2–1 for 13 out of a possible 18 points to start the season. It was near perfection for a franchise so accustomed to failure — and they were doing it in the wake of a great tragedy. That night in Toronto, the Snyders watched the team continue its inspired stretch of winning hockey.

The Snyders attended a pre-game meal hosted for them and about 20 Thrashers personnel by the NHL at a local hotel near the Air Canada Centre. Many who attended that function had helped to organize events before, after or during Snyder's funeral. At the game, in a ploy to avoid television cameras, Graham and LuAnn did not sit together. The ruse did not work for long. In the first period, the Maple Leafs put a message on the scoreboard that read: "To the Snyder family and the Atlanta Thrashers. Over the past few weeks the Toronto Maple Leafs and the people of Toronto have been thinking about you." It was a simple message and fans and players — Maple Leafs Tie Domi and Bryan McCabe had attended Dan Snyder's memorial service — respectfully applauded, the players tapping sticks on the ice or against the boards in front of their benches.

At the time, a crew from ABC's *Good Morning America* was filming the Snyders for a planned segment about how the family had handled Dan's death and embraced Dany Heatley. "They thought they wouldn't have us sit together so no one would find out," LuAnn said. "We were at opposite sides of the arena, and no one knew who we were until right when they flashed that message. That *Good Morning America* crew came over. We were sitting, and [Thrashers public relations director Tom Hughes] sent them over, and the guy started taking my picture. And they flashed that [message] on the scoreboard and I almost swallowed my heart. I was sitting with my sister-in-law and a friend, and another girl from Elmira. . . . I just burst into tears, and people around us figured out what was going on and who we were, and they were very nice to us. The Atlanta cameras were right next to us. They flashed the camera on us a couple of times. The people there were very, very nice."

Covering the Maple Leafs in Toronto is one of the larger media gaggles in North America. Canada had been gripped by the story of Snyder's death, the family's forgiveness of Heatley and the plight of perhaps the country's next great player. Plus, the Thrashers were off to an inexplicably strong start. Toronto newspapers that day were filled with stories about Heatley, Snyder and the team. When Bob Hartley came off the ice after the morning skate to address the media, he was enveloped by a few dozen radio and television reporters, writers and television cameras. The scene was similar after the game. Hartley was asked about the message on the scoreboard. "It was very touching and very appropriate," he said. "Toronto people are classy people, and so is the Maple Leaf organization."

Kovalchuk, who, as recently as the previous season was camera-shy, and at times chose to speak through an interpreter, did not flinch from the attention of the media mob. "We played this game for Dan Snyder and his family," he said. "It was a difficult game for us, but I think he's happy right now."

After the game, the Snyders met up with the team. Bob Hartley showed them Dan's watchband, the gift from LuAnn the night her son died, which Hartley pulled from his pocket. And Kovalchuk, who had just been named NHL player of the week, was effusive. The mercurial young Russian's talent had never been questioned, but now his effort was showing, and he was becoming one of the league's top scorers.

"He came flying out," LuAnn Snyder said. "He said, 'I'm working very hard and I'm working very hard for Dan. I am. I am working very hard.' He really was doing it. He did it for Dan. I don't know how much of an influence I had. He gave me a big kiss and a big hug. 'I'm working very hard, I'm trying very hard.' He did try hard."

The Thrashers suffered their first losing streak, with defeats on back-to-back nights, October 30 at Minnesota, and on October 31 at Washington. But the team remained resilient, as the Thrashers seemed immune to bad luck on the ice — for the time being. Centre Marc Savard, at the time one of the league leaders in scoring, was having a breakout season but before the team travelled to Buffalo it was discovered that Savard had suffered a high-ankle sprain in a 2–2 tie on November 2 at home against San Jose. The injury threatened to keep him out for a couple of months, and for a team already short on manpower at forward with Heatley out, losing Savard could be crippling. On November 5 in Buffalo, the Thrashers trailed 3–1 4:21 into the second period. From there, they scored the next six goals and won 7–4.

On November 8 at the New York Islanders, they fell behind 2–0, went ahead 3–2, and then high-strung goalie Pasi Nurminen allowed a 100-footer to tie the game. But Serge Aubin completed a 2-on-1 for a 4–3 lead with less than nine minutes left in regulation. After that win, the Thrashers' record stood at an impressive 7–4–3–1. But their play had grown sloppy in the games leading up to the win over the Islanders, and that trend spilled over into a losing streak. They lost their next three in a row, falling to .500 for the first time on the season, and were outscored 14–4 in the process, as the defence showed ominous signs of weakness.

Before the losing streak flew out of control, the Thrashers righted themselves, reeling off four straight wins. While modest, it was the longest winning streak in the beleaguered franchise's history. On November 23, Savard returned three weeks to the day he suffered his injury, to score the only goal in a 1-0 win over Phoenix. The miraculous recovery was made possible by an innovative surgical procedure, in which doctors put screws in the player's ankle to help him heal more quickly. The surgery worked like magic.

Later in the week, on American Thanksgiving, Savard would infamously earn a one-game suspension for biting the gloved thumb of Toronto's Darcy Tucker. Said the feisty Savard: "He shoved his fingers in my mouth, so how do you get rid of a mouth hold? The guy's mauling you, you can't breathe. It's like a chokehold. How do you get rid of that, stomp on someone's foot?" The bite meant Savard had to sit out the showdown for first place that Saturday against Tampa Bay, who'd tied the Thrashers for first place in the Southeast Division the night before with a 2–2 tie. The Lightning entered having played only 19 games, the fewest in the league, with 13 of those at home, and the Thrashers having played 24 — tied for the most in the NHL. It was a significant game for a five-year-old franchise which so rarely had anything to play for. The Thrashers scored two third-period goals, the second coming on the power play from J. P. Vigier with 4:57 left in regulation, for a 2–1 victory in a playoff-type atmosphere at Philips Arena. The surprising Thrashers were alone in first place heading into December.

Jake Snyder had lost his brother and his closest friend. Dany Heatley had lost a close friend with the added guilt of feeling some sense of responsibility for it. That formed the basis for a strong bond and mutual dependence, though the two had never met before the accident. "Probably right after the accident and the funeral, I talked to him at least twice a week," Jake said. "Just to talk to see how he was doing, and he would call to see how I was doing. Everyone was pretty concerned about each other at that time. Especially at that time, he was going through all the rehab."

Somehow in the course of one of those conversations, there was an invitation for Jake and Graham to come to Atlanta and stay with Heatley. Graham could only be there for the weekend starting Friday, December 5, but Jake would stay on an additional week. The Friday they arrived, the Thrashers were hosting the Anaheim Mighty Ducks. Graham was anxious to get to the game and see general manager Don Waddell, coach Bob Hartley and the players for the first time in about five weeks. It would be the only game during his brief stay.

His spirits buoyed, Heatley, who had not attended a Thrashers' game all season, drove to the game with Graham, Jake, Heatley's mother and agent Stacey McAlpine. En route, Heatley called Thrashers officials to inform them of his arrival. The group planned to watch the game from a box, but Heatley had not yet spoken to reporters, and in such a forum the team felt they could not protect him if reporters approached him to answer questions.

"I know Dany was going through a really rough time for a while when we got down there," Jake said. "It was the first time he really wanted to go to a game. Maybe if we cleared it with the team they may have went for it. I kind of understand." When they arrived, team officials told Heatley what to expect if he were spotted at the game.

"What we did throughout the whole process was to recommend the best thing for him," Waddell said. "Initially, he thought they could come, sneak in and sneak out, without ever being seen. Our position was, 'Dany, that's not going to happen. You're going to be seen. You've got to be ready for that.' To think you're coming into the arena and you can avoid the media — if the whole idea is that you don't want to be seen — it's pretty difficult to do. We laid it out for him."

Heatley conferred with McAlpine and elected not to go after all. "They were trying to do their job to protect him," Jake said. "It would've been nice to boost his spirits a bit. I know myself and my dad, I felt a lot better going down there, too."

The rest of the week was more casual. Jake sat on the bench during Thrashers' practices while Heatley was rehabbing with assistant trainer Craig Brewer. Joey Guilmet, the team's assistant equipment manager and Dan's good friend, outfitted Jake with goalie pads left behind by departed players like Damian Rhodes and Milan Hnilicka. One day after practice, Jake took shots from Ben Simon and Jeff Cowan.

"It went all right," Jake said. "I'm not in as good a shape as I used to be, even compared to five years ago. I got winded more than I thought I would. They're passing and I'm doing side-to-side across the crease, taking shots. When I warm up for church league on Thursday nights, I take five shots, and then I see 20 or 30 in the game. Games are always different than practice. You've got to be in shape for practice." That week, goalie Byron Dafoe was in the process of getting his U.S. citizenship and showed up late for practice one day. Jake would have acted as one of the goalies during practice if Dafoe had shown up too late. "I was a little disappointed," Jake said.

The Ontario Hockey League's Owen Sound franchise, known as the Attack by 2003, had given Ryan Christie about a month's notice to prepare a recorded audio statement for the night the club would retire Dan Snyder's number. Christie had joined Owen Sound the same year as Snyder, and they became line-mates and then the best of friends. Christie could not be present, as his East Coast Hockey League team, the Las Vegas Wranglers, would be in Alaska the night of the ceremony. Some members of the franchise's broadcast team supplied Christie with the recording equipment and left him alone in a room.

"It took about eight tries," he said. "I was probably in there for half an hour or 45 minutes. I wrote it all out and I was trying to read it. That was pretty tough, but I finally got it out. It was probably as good as it was going to get." During his month to prepare, Christie would write something down every time a thought struck him as significant. "I wanted everyone to hear how I felt he was as a person," Christie said. "I think that got out. I wanted to express how I thought every-body else felt, and I knew how they felt in Owen Sound about him. . . . It's too bad it always takes a tragedy like that for some-one to get recognized, but that's what happens all the time."

In the days before Owen Sound held the ceremony on December 19, the Thrashers had continued their streaky play, losing those three games by the combined score of 12–0. Still, they remained in first in the Southeast Division ahead of Tampa Bay, who were struggling through their most difficult stretch of the season, with coach John Tortorella and star centre Vincent Lecavalier poised for a public spat in the coming days.

Though his team was barely treading water, Thrashers general manager Don Waddell could still say that his team was in first place at the ceremony in Owen Sound. In his brief remarks, he credited Dan Snyder for the team's achievements.

"We can talk about Dan in so many different ways," he said. "It's unbelievable. Words can't explain what he meant to our hockey team. Not just prior to his death, but right now. We know he can't be with us in body, but he sits with us in our locker room. Every day. I know our guys are very proud to have him as a teammate and, more importantly, as a friend. I know our hockey club, we're sitting in first place, and it is because of Dan Snyder."

During the ceremony, OHL commissioner David Branch talked about how, one month earlier, the league's governors had voted unanimously to rename its humanitarian award for Snyder, who had twice been named the Owen Sound team's humanitarian of the year. That night, it was also mentioned that the high school Snyder graduated from in Owen Sound, West Hill Secondary School, had named its award for the athlete who excels in sports outside of school programs after Snyder.

The most impassioned speech at the ceremony came from Christie. As his recording was played over the arena's sound system, the delivery of the 6-foot-4 Christie — nicknamed

"Sticks" for being stick skinny — was flat, a bit of a monotone and somewhat halting. At times one could discern the choking and trembling of his voice, still the elegance of his words rang clear.

"I wish I could be there to share in the honour being given in the memory of my friend, Dan Snyder," he began. "He was drafted in Owen Sound in 1995, the same year as I was. That was when I first met Dan. We were both rookies and we were linemates. During the three years I played in Owen Sound, we were inseparable. Dan grew up in Elmira and I grew up in Beamsville, both small towns about an hour from each other. Perhaps it was our roots in growing up in small farming communities. I remember that we always teased one another about which small town was best. And we spent every summer travelling back and forth to each other's homes. Dan's friends and family became mine, and mine became his. We shared our most special secrets, our hopes, dreams, triumphs and setbacks. We stayed in touch no matter where we were living. My last conversation with Dan was him excitedly saying, 'Sticks, they told me to find a place to live.' He had made it.

"Dan was a good person, a great teammate and a greater friend. What made him so special? There are many things. He was fun, caring, mischievous. He had a strong and free spirit. He worked hard and never gave up. His hockey career speaks for itself. He had a dream and he made you believe dreams could come true. He never doubted his abilities and made believers out of others. Dan touched so many others in so many ways. He would always take the time to listen.

"The love between siblings has been described as unequalled. Jake and Erika will always feel a void. A parent's love for a child is unyielding, uncompromising and special, and I know Graham and LuAnn will never be the same without Dan in their world. I can tell you from my experiences with Dan, the Atlanta Thrashers lost a great teammate. Owen Sound is a better place because it had Dan as a member of the community. The organization should feel honoured that Dan's jersey will be hanging in the rafters of the Bayshore Centre. I am a better person for having known Dan. I was lucky to have the good fortune of playing with him, learning from him and being his friend. I will cherish the many memories we made over the last eight years. I would like to think that Dan lives on in the lives that he touched. They say nothing loved is ever lost, and he was loved very much. Snydes, I miss you."

One day in the week before Christmas, the Snyders heard a knock at the door. On her front steps, LuAnn instantly recognized a familiar face — but it was someone she had never met in person, the CBC's Ron MacLean. Through his "Coach's Corner" segment with Don Cherry on *Hockey Night in Canada*, MacLean is one of Canada's most recognizable people. The broadcaster had been touched by the Snyders' forgiveness of Dany Heatley, and wanted to speak with them in person.

After being ushered into their home, MacLean instantly found an affection for the family dog, Spike, a Yorkshire Terrier who was then 13 years old. An owner of a Schnauzer himself, MacLean found amusement in one of Spike's toys, a stuffed bear wearing a purple suit in the color of the Anaheim Mighty Ducks, with "Kariya" printed on the back.

MacLean wanted to present the family with something that was meaningful to him. So now, sitting in their television room on the mantle to the right of the fireplace, not far from framed action photos of Dan from his playing career is a Gemini Award presented to MacLean. The award, Canada's equivalent of the Emmys in the United States, has a plaque that reads: "16th Annual Gemini Awards: Best Broadcast, NHL."

Graham Snyder had met MacLean for the first time in the weeks following the accident, a time when Graham's brother Jeff had handled many of the media inquiries on the family's behalf. MacLean and Don Cherry had attended the funeral in Elmira, but in the small church, there were not enough seats available, so they stood outside and listened on a loudspeaker. On the opening *Hockey Night in Canada* broadcast of the season, MacLean spoke directly into the camera to Jake Snyder, expressing admiration for what Jake had said at his brother's memorial service. Later that summer, when the Snyders organized a golf tournament to benefit charities they designated in Dan's memory, MacLean was unable to attend because he had a sailing trip scheduled. But he went so far as to try and rearrange his vacation so he might attend. The Snyders had wanted MacLean to serve as master of ceremonies. In the end, TSN's Bob MacKenzie filled in in his place.

MacKenzie had made a commentary in defence of Dany Heatley in reaction to a controversial column by the *Toronto Star*'s Mary Ormsby, who'd referred to Heatley as "just a punk in a fast car" — words that offended the Snyders. "He had some pretty strong words to say," Graham said of the commentary. "I know Jeff [Snyder] was really pleased. . . . I've never known for sure what happened that night [the night of the accident]. . . . But if I'm going to be wrong, it's going to be thinking the best of someone."

A short while after MacLean's visit, Graham and LuAnn

were spending some holiday time with relatives of LuAnn in Chatham, and were half asleep watching *Hockey Night in Canada*. MacLean came on air and apologized for not having any news on the sledge hockey team coached by Graham's brother Jeff. He then said, "Speaking of the Snyders, I've got something for you." Then he rolled a clip showing Paul Kariya, still playing for the Ducks, scoring on a penalty shot.

By December 10, Thrashers general manager Don Waddell had said that Dany Heatley would begin skating within two weeks. Given that it was just over two months since Heatley had had his surgery, he was on a remarkable timetable to return. When doctors went into his knee during the reconstruction, they found a completely torn anterior cruciate ligament, a completely torn medial collateral ligament and another partially torn ligament. They took a tendon from Heatley's left knee to help to repair the right one.

Five days later, Waddell announced early in the afternoon that Heatley would skate for the first time the next day. A few hours later, he would have to issue a retraction, citing soreness in Heatley's knee. For someone like Waddell, who had pursued a cautious path throughout Heatley's rehabilitation to avoid such situations, this was slightly embarrassing. Nonetheless, the general manager danced around the issue of whether Heatley had suffered a setback.

"He's been working out and everything's been fine," Waddell said. "He's a little bit sore. The next step, as we talked about, was going on the ice. It wasn't a big issue, but it was big enough to say, 'Let's delay it.'"

Two days before Christmas, Heatley took to the ice for the first time since the accident. The setting was somewhat surreal: the rest of the team was off the ice, the media were invited for the highly anticipated event and television cameras captured it, but Heatley did not answer questions afterwards. Here was an alien forum for a hockey player — no teammates, no opponents, no drills; it was as if he were performing a cathartic role in a maudlin ballet about the ill-fated turns of his life. About a hundred fans were present, who applauded Heatley as he took to the ice. Some of his teammates had also come out to watch. About 10 minutes into the session, Heatley smiled at a young fan.

"It's an emotional lift for everyone," Waddell said. "But the healing process is ongoing. It just doesn't happen overnight. Until he is back playing, we won't see the real Dany. He's dealt with a lot, but he still has a lot to deal with."

At that moment, Waddell spoke for Heatley. But in three days — the day after Christmas — Heatley would speak for himself for the first time.

The night of December 26 was almost like something scripted for a movie. Dany Heatley attended his first Thrashers game in a private box with his family; the Thrashers beat the Tampa Bay Lightning 3-1 to give themselves an eight-point lead in the Southeast Division; and the team was five games over .500 for just the second time in franchise history. Only 45 games remained in the season. For the first time, playoffs for this Atlanta franchise seemed a definite possibility.

Three hours before the start of the game, Dany Heatley did

something that would be more difficult than anything he'd ever done on a hockey rink. Behind one of the sections of club seating in Philips Arena, the Thrashers set up a stage backed with black curtains. Having been alerted several days in advance, the major Canadian networks were all present. Altogether, several dozen reporters were there.

The event began with Heatley walking onstage by himself and sitting down alone. He made a brief statement, then answered his first questions about the accident, nearly three months after the fact. It did not seem possible that the famous gap-toothed grin could emanate from the same person, Heatley was so sombre. The answers he gave are among the most emotional he has made, as to how the accident affected him. He began with a statement about his friend: "I'm very sorry and deeply saddened by the loss of my teammate and friend Danny Snyder. He was a great guy in the locker room, a great person. I miss him in the locker room and forever. . . . As a person, I'll never be the same," he said. "This has changed me, and it will change me down the road."

Citing legal advice, Heatley could not answer questions about the accident, or whether he felt responsible. His lawyer, Ed Garland, and general manager Don Waddell would speak after Heatley was done. At the time of Heatley's news conference, the public was unaware that a concussion negated any memory Heatley might have had of the night of the accident. When asked repeatedly about Snyder, Heatley chose to closely guard his thoughts, as he has ever since. Nonetheless, he described the profound effect Snyder's death had upon him.

"It's a private thing," he said, his voice choking with emotion. "I'm going to deal with this forever. Every time I go to sleep I think about Dan. It'll be with me for the rest of my life." He was asked which was more difficult, his physical or emotional injuries. "They've both been tough. Emotionally, that's been the most draining and most tough thing to get through. The people around me have been unbelievable. The Snyders have been unbelievable. They have given me a lot of strength."

At the time of the accident, Heatley was on the verge of becoming one of the world's premiere players. Would he be the same?

"As a player I'd like to think I will be," he said. "As a person, I don't think you can ever be the same. This has changed me. It will change me down the road. But you have to go on and try to deal with things the best you can."

CHAPTER 8

THE MENNONITES AND RESTORATIVE JUSTICE

Every other Sunday, a little bit after 9 a.m., horse-drawn carriages ramble through the sloping hills of Woolwich Township towards the town of Elmira. The closer they get to their destination, the more congested grow the town's picturesque streets with the black buggies — the Old Order Mennonites' antique mode of transportation that still somehow does not quite look out of place. When the drivers reach the meeting house on Church Street, they orchestrate their horses in a sort of extended line dance so they can park the vehicles in an orderly fashion.

The horse and buggies are just one example of how the Old Order Mennonites eschew many modern ways. The Old Order sect is somewhat similar to their Mennonite brethren, the Amish, who are perhaps better known in the United

States, where they live in large numbers in Lancaster County, Pennsylvania, and have become something of a tourist industry there. Both sects developed during the second half of the 18th century, as schisms within existing orders. There were also schisms within schisms, and Woolwich is home to several different sects of Mennonites. The Old Order was founded in the United States in 1872 by Jacob Wisler, who, according to the Mennonite Historical Society of Canada, "was opposed to any change in the life of the church" at that time. Abraham Martin, born near St. Jacobs, Ontario, in Woolwich Township, is considered the father of the Canadian Old Order movement, having made his break in 1889.

Inside the Old Order meeting house in Elmira, the service is performed in a dialect of German — Pennsylvania Dutch. The Woolwich Mennonites are descended from Swiss Mennonites who had been invited by the Quaker William Penn when he founded his colony based on ideals of religious tolerance and freedom. About 100 years later, around the time of the American Revolution, those Swiss Mennonites arrived on their Conestoga wagons in Canada in search of cheaper land. Dan's grandfather Joseph Snyder, who is something of a hobbyist in genealogy, said his ancestors arrived in Canada from Pennsylvania in 1806.

In the 1920s, many Mennonites began to leave the Old Order to embrace more modern ways and new technology. Among them were Joseph Snyder's parents. Their departure from the Old Order came as a result of their decision to own a telephone and an automobile. Although he was born two years after his parents left the Old Order, Joseph Snyder, the youngest of seven children, was raised speaking German, and did not learn English until he entered school. He raised Graham in the

Elmira Mennonite Church and Graham brought his children — Jake, Dan and Erika — to the simple brick building, which has a present-day congregation of 325 members.

The church sits just on the opposite side of a fence from the meeting house where the Old Orders gather, and the congregations share a common cemetery, where Dan is buried. Graham Snyder, born and raised in Elmira, is a member of the Elmira Mennonite Church. However, LuAnn was raised in the United Church and is not a Mennonite, and none of her children were baptized — an important distinction. To become a member of the church, individuals must make the decision to be baptized. Usually, teenagers or young adults choose to become members when they feel they are ready for the commitment. By their own admission, the Snyders are not what one might call "religious" people.

LuAnn Snyder prefers to talk about her spirituality, as opposed to her religion. While neither Jake, nor Dan nor Erika were baptized, they were "dedicated" upon birth — a ceremony in which the parents declare their intention to raise their child in a Christian environment. The Snyder children also attended Sunday school. In a further sign of that spirituality, after Dan died, LuAnn sought counselling from the Elmira Mennonite Church's minister, Ruth Anne Laverty. So when LuAnn and her family had to confront the tragedy of Dan's death, it was no surprise when they fell back on values that had been inculcated over so many years — regardless of how often the family might have attended church.

Throughout her family's ordeal, LuAnn Snyder says reporters have wondered how her family has forgiven Dany Heatley. Her answer is that it was never a conscious decision. She remains unsure of the extent to which Mennonite beliefs

— among the most important of which are pacifism and for-giveness — might have influenced the family's actions. But she also won't deny it.

"I don't know," she says in answer to the question. "I really couldn't answer that one way or another. For Graham, that was the way he was raised. It was ingrained. I shouldn't say it was not the way I was raised. It was the way I was raised, but I wasn't in the Mennonite Church. That's the way we are because of the community we're in. It's like osmosis. That's how the people are here, and that's the way you do it. . . . It doesn't seem like an oddity to us. That's the way we are.

"We don't [question it] because that's the makeup of who we are and what we are, and how it got that way is beyond me. With reporters especially, they'll ask, 'At what point in time did you decide to forgive Dany Heatley?' It wasn't a point in time. It was a given. That's what you do. They look at you like you have six heads. 'Why haven't you called six lawyers?' Even people in Elmira have said, 'You have more temerity than we do. We don't know if we could've done it.' But how do you know until you're faced with it? . . . That's the most common question we've been asked. It's no different than saying, 'How are your eyes blue?' Well, that's how I was born. I did get a gene from each parent, but I'm my own person. We all think the same. . . . We've never felt any different."

Ruth Anne Laverty, the Snyders' minister, believes religion and culture have a powerful effect on how values are shaped, regardless of how conscious one might be of dogma. "We learn our values during our formative years, but in adolescence we may react against what we have learned," she said. "Most of us question it, but don't move too far away. These things would've been reinforced regularly, at home and through our Christian Education Program. They're very important values and when both home and church have similar values the child gets congruence and reinforcement. And that's very powerful. Even when people rebel they too are attached to their values. They express them differently."

Laverty was neither a native of Woolwich Township, nor born into the Mennonite faith. Laverty, who exudes warmth and a maternal compassion, has great tresses of slightly graying red hair. She has several degrees and speaks carefully and thoughtfully. And she has lived through what she calls "a grief experience" herself. In 1968, Laverty was in Bolivia when she received a call telling her to return home to Canada because her father had died unexpectedly. Several weeks later, her mother suffered a massive stroke and never spoke again.

She was studying for her master of arts at what was then Waterloo Lutheran University (now Wilfrid Laurier). She and her husband, Brian, whom she describes as having lost his faith, rented an apartment from a Mennonite family, who had Amish Mennonite roots and lived near the rural community of Tavistock.

"They were friendly and warm and provided us with love and support," Laverty said. "Having lost much of my family, I thought it was great." The family invited Ruth Anne and her husband to attend church with them and they took up the offer.

"We were two former teachers from the city of Toronto living in this rural community that had Amish Mennonite roots," Laverty said. "The East Zorra church community and their pastor received us very warmly, and we began to feel a part of that community as we made friendships there. . . . My husband also refound his faith in that community. That sense of community was so powerful. So that's how we got into the Mennonite Church. Through seeing love in action amongst those Mennonites in that community we got to see it's possible to live a life of faith and peace — not just talk about it. To actually put it to action." Today, Ruth Anne's husband, Brian, is a minister at Pioneer Park Christian Fellowship, a Mennonite Church in nearby Kitchener.

According to the 2001 census, six-tenths of one percent of Canadians were Mennonite: 191,465, to be exact. That is about one-thirteenth the population of Toronto. It's also a smaller percentage of Canada's population than those who are Greek Orthodox, Sikh, Hindu, Buddhist or Jewish. Almost one-third of Canada's Mennonites live in Ontario with others, notably immigrants from Eastern Europe, spread out over Western Canada. In 1807, the Swiss Mennonite Benjamin Eby founded what is now Kitchener, the largest city in Ontario's Waterloo Region, which itself has one of Canada's largest Mennonite concentrations. In comparison, the United States is home to only slightly more Mennonites, about 346,000. Again, that is also a tiny fraction of the American population: one-tenth of one percent, according to the American Religious Identification Survey of 2001. Most American Mennonites live in Pennsylvania, Indiana, Ohio and Virginia's Shenandoah Valley.

The sect came out of the Anabaptist movement early during the Protestant Reformation. (Although there is considerable debate among religious experts as to who exactly is Anabaptist, a basic definition would be those who believed either in the rebaptizing of people who were baptized as infants, or those who did not believe in baptizing infants.) The Mennonite sect dates itself as early as January 21, 1525, when it was founded in what is now northern Switzerland by Felix Muntz and Conrad Grable, after whom a university is named in Waterloo. The Mennonite name comes from Menno Simons, a one-time Benedictine monk who believed Christians should not be baptized until they reached an age of responsibility. Today, the age varies when young adults choose to be baptized and become members of the church.

"It's up to them," Laverty said. "There's no pressure for people to be baptized at a particular age."

Aside from their theological beliefs about baptism, social justice and pacificism are preeminent Mennonite tenets. During World War II, many Mennonites were conscientious objectors. Joseph Snyder, although too young himself to be drafted during World War II, knew many conscientious objectors.

"There were a number of them that went to work camps," he said. "Some from here went to British Columbia to work, and some went up to Sault Ste. Marie, building roads. They had to apply for it [conscientious objector status] and so on. Most of them didn't have a hard time getting it. A lot of them were Mennonites, but they weren't all. The majority were."

In 1539, Menno Simons offered this in relation to his pacificism: "The regenerated do not go to war nor engage in strife. They are the children of peace who have beaten their swords into plowshares and their spears into pruning hooks and know of no war. . . . Since we are to be conformed to Christ, how can we then fight our enemies with the sword?"

That reluctance to take up the sword applies not just to militarism but to criminal justice.

From the day Dany Heatley was indicted by a Fulton County grand jury, District Attorney Paul Howard talked about the need for Heatley to be "accountable." In the Snyders' eyes, he was from the start. The Snyders' minister says that the way the family has reacted towards Heatley fits in with the Mennonites' concept of a "peace witness" and the religion's call for social justice. Ruth Anne Laverty quoted Christ's famous passage from Matthew, Chapter 18 Verse 22. "We forgive each other," she said. "Jesus said, 'How many times must we forgive? Not seven times but seventy times seven.' He called for us to forgive others for what they do to us. [The belief] is a big one, but it doesn't mean people get off scot free. It means accountability, as well. Forgiveness, not retaliation, not going for revenge is very important to us as Mennonites. . . . Instead of packing people off to jail, we try to bring reconciliation."

Laverty jokes that she has had three vocations. Before she became a minister, she was a teacher. In addition to being a minister, she was also a marriage therapist. In her counselling sessions with the Snyders, Laverty said she simply tried to listen.

"I don't say a whole lot. I just try to be present with people and listen," she said. "There's not a whole lot to say. [It helps] just to be present and listen over and over again and for people to talk about it. . . . Each time you tell your story, it releases some of your feelings. Being able to laugh and cry releases your feelings. I try to do active listening to see where the person is coming from."

She talks about "walking with" the Snyders through their

Photography by Picture Yourself

Dan's Woolwich Township Major Novice team photo, 1987–88

Jake and Dan in 1983

Christmas: Dan wearing his favourite Nordiques hat

Grade 8 graduation: with the awards for all-around student, athlete and citizen

Dan, Jake and Erika on holiday at Busch Gardens, 1987

Dan after the annual Woolwich Township tournament, 1990

Dan's Burger King player card, from his first year with the Owen Sound Platers, 1995

Dan and Jake — with wild hair

Jake, Erika and Dan, 1998

Like father like son: Graham and Dan remove their teeth to celebrate the Wolves winning the Calder Cup

Dan lifts the Turner Cup, 2001 — also pictured is Orlando Solar Bears teammate and friend, Jarrod Skalde

With the Turner Cup: Curtis Murphy, Dan Snyder, Jim Hughes and Bryan Adams

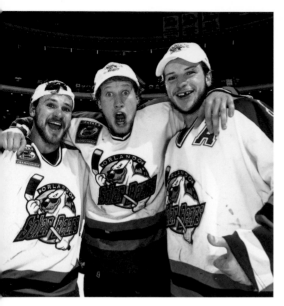

*Curtis, Bryan and Dan celebrate
on the ice*

Dan on the bench during the playoffs

*Dan with his sister Erika in a headlock, and celebrating back-to-back cups
at a party in Elmira*

The Snyder grandchildren, 2002

Dan with the Thrashers

Celebrating a goal

Dan Snyder and Dany Heatley

Dan and Jeff Odgers

Dan Snyder

"Snydes, Forever in our Hearts."

"grief experience"; something she calls "spirit-soul connected-ness." "Losing a child is a tremendous grief experience. I can hardly imagine what that can be like. [Sudden death] is not part of what we expect in that developmental stage of life. There is a part of our human nature that wants justice. For me, going for revenge or retaliation doesn't bring about heal-ing. It's about not bringing about more pain so that healing can happen. There's a whole lot of violence out there in our culture. It takes someone who can have a greater vision than what's happening right now at this moment. [Revenge] comes from the futility that comes with remaining angry. We all have anger, but it's how we chose to express it. We can choose to express our feelings productively and be constructive or we can choose unhealthy ways which creates more pain. [Forgiveness] is productive rather than destructive."

In modern life in the Western World, life expectancy is more than seven decades, and many people might not be touched personally by the untimely death of parent, child or loved one. Laverty does not believe that going through life without experiencing a tragedy is simply a matter of luck.

"I see it as an unmerited blessing we receive from God," she said. "However, in the midst of pain, we see or experience another side of life. I think pain is a part of life. I don't blame God because I don't think God causes us pain. Rather, it's the fragility of life. Some people see more and some see less pain." Laverty thinks it's possible that this unmerited blessing, as she calls it, is underappreciated and that tragedy acts as a reminder of the fragility of life.

"Pain is a part of our humanity," she said. "We're all vul-nerable whether we are aware of it or not."

In a little known way, unassuming Elmira — a town of just over 7,000 people — was the crucible for an experiment in social justice that has had repercussions throughout the world. In 1974, two youths went on a drunken rampage in the town, slashing tires, vandalizing churches and generally damaging property. Police apprehended the pair and their case was assigned to Mark Yantzi, a Mennonite who had been assigned years earlier by the church's volunteer arm, the Mennonite Central Committee, to work as a probation officer in nearby Kitchener, home of the Waterloo Region courts. The Mennonite Central Committee, according to its Web site, is a relief, service and peace agency that "reflects the biblical call to care for the hungry and thirsty, the stranger, the sick and those in prison." As a volunteer, the MCC paid Yantzi's living expenses and he donated his salary back to it. Five years after he began working in the probation office in Kitchener, Yantzi had a bit of an epiphany. Drawing upon his religious beliefs, Yantzi, the son of a Mennonite minister, decided there might be a way to apply justice that didn't involve "grinding the boys through the criminal justice system," as he put it. But even he had some doubts. Having worked as long as he had in the probation office, he knew the law had little room for revolutionary ideas. Yantzi met regularly with other volunteers from the Mennonite Central Committee, and one in particular, Dave Worth, was instrumental in convincing him to follow through and put his ideas into his pre-sentence report.

When the case was called before Ontario Provincial Court Judge Gordon McConnell, Yantzi approached the bench and asked to speak to him in his chambers. There, he pointed out his pre-sentencing ideas and asked if there were ways he could monitor the boys as they made restitution, without their having to be incarcerated. McConnell said initially that he could not do it, that the crimes were not against the victims, they were against the state. But when they returned to the courtroom, McConnell took the unusual step of saying he wanted to take some time with the case. To the shock of those in the room, he allowed Yantzi to implement his ideas.

"I was enough ingrained in the system [to know] that that didn't happen," said Yantzi, who went on to work as a city councilman in Kitchener. "It would've ended there except that the volunteers [from the Mennonite Central Committee] said, 'Let's do something.' I knew the system and could build a way to make it happen, but I couldn't do it without their encouragement. You tend to have blinders on once you know a system."

Yantzi and Worth began by bringing the boys to the places they had vandalized. They knocked on doors and the boys were forced to face the victims of their crimes. They made financial restitution for damaged property, and when McConnell reconvened the case, Yantzi presented evidence of cashiers' checks that the boys had given to their victims. The judge was satisfied and the case was adjudicated without either ever being incarcerated. Thus, the Waterloo Community Justice Initiatives was born, and with it, victim-offender reconciliation programs (VORPs), which offer mediation and conflict resolution outside the criminal justice system. Today, hundreds of such programs exist, from local jurisdictions in Canada and the United States, to Australia, New Zealand and across Europe. In Kitchener, one of the original offenders in the Elmira case, Russell Kelly, now works for the Waterloo Criminal Justice Initiatives, and is a model of the program's success.

Dean Peachey chronicled the "Elmira Case," as it has become known, in an essay entitled "The Kitchener Experiment." He is a Mennonite from Pennsylvania who has lived and worked in Canada for almost 30 years. Peachey, who now works at Menno Simons College in Winnipeg, has researched mediation with Yantzi and cowritten a manual on the subject. His original interest in exploring what is known as restorative justice — reconciliation as opposed to incarceration — came during the turbulent Vietnam era in the United States. He wanted to see how pacifism could be implemented, not just in opposing war, but in everyday applications in the criminal justice system. Peachey points out that nothing happens in a vacuum, and that at the time of Yantzi's epiphany similar thinking was going on elsewhere with regard to victim-offender programs. (However, Elmira and Kitchener may have represented the perfect storm for the first such program to come about.) And the Elmira Case is often credited with providing the impetus for the birth of these programs.

"Without the Mennonite Central Committee's support and so forth, I doubt Mark Yantzi would end up in a probation office, I doubt he thinks outside the box and raises this question, 'Why not?'" Peachey said. "What does peacemaking have to say to the criminal justice system? It emerged directly from Mennonite understandings, but those aren't unique."

Ideas have many ways of rubbing off. First, one must be exposed to them, as Ruth Anne Laverty was when she lived with a Mennonite family. In the case of Graham and LuAnn Snyder, those ideas might have been introduced in church, but they also encountered them in their community. And not just in Elmira. In something of a coincidence, Graham and LuAnn Snyder knew Mark Yantzi around the time of his epiphany. In fact, they were married in Yantzi's home. When she first moved east with Graham, LuAnn rented an apartment in Kitchener that backed onto property where Yantzi lived. Although they lost touch over the years, Yantzi — who has written pieces in the Kitchener newspaper about violence in hockey — sent Graham a condolence card after Dan died. A phone call ensued and then a meeting. Yantzi said he saw what the Snyders had done as consistent with Mennonite faith, and he offered support and encouragement.

"As a society, we've bought into this punishment thing that is so destructive," Yantzi said. "No matter what you do, how much you ratchet up. But if people take responsibility and back away from punishment, and say, 'What can we do to address these needs and encourage and support the offender and do something that's right?' I said to Graham, 'I don't know the judicial system in Georgia well, but I think that there's so many possibilities for something constructive to come out of this.' A punitive sanction adds so much pain, nothing positive."

Yantzi thought there was a potential for restorative justice to work in Heatley's case. "I would encourage them to say to the state not to prosecute [Heatley]. But that's very Mennonite, too, to be involved in the system and not tell them what to do."

In "The Kitchener Experiment," Dean Peachey elaborated on that concept when explaining how revolutionary Yantzi's work was as a probation officer. "To be so directly tied to a part of the criminal justice system was itself an experiment for him as a Mennonite: the church had traditionally maintained a separation from governmental affairs, and particularly from the legal system with its reliance on coercive power," Peachey wrote.

Yantzi feared the courts might make an example of Heatley. "Part of the problem is that, because it's such a high-profile case, the system is sensitive to not making an exception. But it cries out for a circle [involving] all the people affected, to sit down and talk about what happened and what could be done. In the NHL, young players go from paupers to multi-millionaires, and management of finances and the pressure of being a teenager or young person and suddenly being so famous, it brings with it a sense of invincibility. You're invincible and you tend to think, too, nothing could ever happen.

"It just seems so much good could come of this in a positive way. The thought of having him incarcerated just for the sake of being consistent — like it's going to achieve anything — instead of being incarcerated in house arrest and have his salary go to a cause that addresses the issues that led to his involvement in this tragic incident. That seems much more restorative. One of the criticisms I have of the justice system is that it's what we've done in the past that governs what happens in future, [but] with little thought to whether what has happened in the past has worked. We keep doing it in the future. His presence at the funeral, it just says he has some understanding of what he's done and he wants to make it right. It's a tough spot for the system to respond to in a creative way. [But] there are excellent opportunities to provide some kind of healing and closure."

Some of the central tenets of the Mennonite religion are summed up in the story of an ancient Anabaptist martyr —

which also is a favourite story of Ruth Anne Laverty. In 1569, Dirk Willems of Asperen, Holland was apprehended by local authorities for being rebaptized, helping to rebaptize others and, in short, going against the doctrines of the Pope. At the time, Holland was ruled by Spain, which acted as one of the Catholic Church's chief instruments in rooting out heretics, lending its name to the infamous Spanish Inquisition. According to "Martyr's Mirror," which was translated into English in 1660, Willems escaped from the place where he was being held, and was pursued.

During the chase, one of the captors fell through some ice covering a small body of water, and Willems returned to save the man's life. When Willems was brought before the local burgomaster, the man whose life was saved asked that Willems be spared. The burgomaster refused and Willems was burned at the stake and was said to suffer an agonizing death.

The fact that Willems' story remains powerful to Mennonites shows the strength of their belief in social justice — that a man who saved his oppressor's life was punished despite his good deed.

"That's a wonderful story," Ruth Anne Laverty said. "I know it's very significant for us as a church. We even created a banner with that picture of Willems pulling on his captor out of the icy water and we hung it up in the church. It reminds us to reach out to others and not to be vengeful. Dirk could have walked away and let him drown in the water. It ended up being a big risk, because he lost his life. It's about turning the other cheek. He could have said, 'Tough to you, you were coming after me in revenge so you can die.' It very graphically illustrates justice and reconciliation. I think that's what Jesus says to us in the Lord's prayer, 'Forgive us our sins as we forgive those who sinned against us.' It's about making a right relationship, even when you are threatened. We talk about having a ministry of reconciliation, trying to reconcile with those who have hurt us in some ways with their words or actions."

The Snyders are not theological experts in the area of reconciliation. They are not students of the criminal justice system trying to reinvent what they perceive as an overly punitive system. Nonetheless, they are everyday people who put those concepts to work at an impossibly difficult time.

"You could tell in the hospital we all felt it — we've got to rally around this boy [Dany Heatley] and let him know we forgive him and we've got to do it now," LuAnn Snyder said. "No one else really mattered. It was letting him know. That was all that mattered to us. It was something we didn't have to ask for the strength to have, or take a poll. We just instantly felt the same way.

"The kids, too, said, 'Yeah, of course. We've got to let him know.' They went down [to see him] on a regular basis when he was in the same hospital. It was a long, lonely ride for him, too. That's what's there in our heart. We felt, too, from a point of view that we feel strongly, it was an accident. I go by the word *intent*. The *intent* was to eat something, get in the vehicle and go home, and get up and do whatever. Nowhere were intentions to have a car accident and get Dan critically injured. He was the driver, but those were not his *intentions*. If someone is going out to rob a bank and they bring a gun, but they only *intend* to use it if they have to and someone gets in their way and they shoot them, there was intention there. I might be a little bit ticked-off and reacting different, if there was intent to what happened. Dany didn't intend for Dan to be so seriously injured. He didn't intend for him to die. That's the way we have to look at it. That's an important word for me: intent. He was the driver and ultimately responsible. But he didn't intend for that to happen."

CHAPTER
9

A RETURN TO THE ICE

The New Year did not start auspiciously for the Thrashers. They lost a sloppy defensive game at Detroit on New Year's Eve in overtime 6–5 — their fourth straight defeat after the victory over Tampa Bay the day after Christmas. Perhaps more damaging than the loss of any single game was the broken foot that stalwart defenceman Andy Sutton suffered against the Red Wings. The injuries were starting to mount: overachieving winger Jeff Cowan suffered a concussion in a fight on December 13 against the New York Islanders' Eric Cairns, and was out for a prolonged period. Steady centre Serge Aubin had a scary incident in Pittsburgh on December 20, going head first into the boards and suffering a concussion and a neck strain.

Two more players went out on January 3 at Montreal, another loss. Fourth-liner Bill Lindsay, a popular player in the locker room, suffered a freak injury when he was hit in the throat with the puck. He would miss the rest of the season. And the injury bug again hit centre Marc Savard, who ranked among the league's leaders in scoring after finishing December with an NHL-best 25 points. The 5-foot-10 Savard, one of the team's most integral players, suffered a concussion when he received an elbow to the head from Canadiens defenceman Sheldon Souray, a 6–4 physical specimen. All the while, Heatley was skating on his own, working with coach Bob Hartley after the team left the ice when the Thrashers were at home, and rehabbing with strength and conditioning coach Ray Bear, trainer Scott Green and his assistant Craig Brewer, who had been assigned Heatley as his special project.

Heatley did not travel with the team as they headed west in early January for three games in four days at Dallas, San Jose and Phoenix. The injuries made the Thrashers desperate for players. They claimed forward Jean-Luc Grand-Pierre off waivers from Columbus, one of the worst teams in the league, and almost immediately pressed him into duty at his former position of defence. In a 2–1 loss to Dallas, the Thrashers, using a lineup featuring three call-ups from the minors and Grand-Pierre, managed only seven shots in the final two periods, and went the first 15 minutes of the third without one. The wheels were starting to fall off the proverbial wagon. The next day, ESPN ran a report saying Heatley would return to play on February 10 at his native Calgary, which would prove off the mark by almost two weeks. The next day in San Jose, the Thrashers fell behind 3–0 less than seven minutes into the game. They had fallen behind by at least 2–0 for the sixth straight game — all losses — and slipped back to the .500 mark. The loss to the Sharks knocked them out of first place for the first time since November 29. Just as the Thrashers were mired in their season-worst losing streak, the Lightning began a surge that would not end until they captured the Stanley Cup.

One day after losing to San Jose, the Thrashers faced a Phoenix team that was riding goalie Brian Boucher's NHL-record shutout streak. Miraculously, Randy Robitaille ended it 6:16 into the first period, with the streak culminating at 332 mintues, 1 second — more than five and a half games. The 1–1 final ended the Thrashers' losing streak, but extended a winless streak to 16 days. Also, dependable veteran defenceman Chris Tamer, the franchise's all-time leader in games played to that point, hurt his back and would play just one more game the rest of the season. Returning home, Aubin was activated for a Wednesday game against Montreal, only to find himself unable to go minutes before the game. Savard, in his first game back, suffered a knee sprain in a collision with the Canadiens' Mike Komisarek during the 2–1 loss. Whereas once the Thrashers could do nothing wrong on the ice, everything seemed to go against them.

Some might say the Thrashers were waiting for Heatley to return and act as their saviour to help end all of the losing. But those expectations were unrealistic. When he would be able to return was unknown and, perhaps more importantly, so was the level he might play at. Would he instantly return as a world-class player? It was doubtful. On the morning of January 16 on the day the Thrashers were to host the Carolina Hurricanes at Philips Arena, Heatley skated with his teammates for the first time since the accident. He wore a red practice jersey — signifying to his teammates that he was off limits to contact. That day was another major milestone in his recovery, even if Heatley did not take part in contact drills and did not address the media afterwards. After the morning skate, Ilya Kovalchuk quipped that Heatley looked as if he were ready to play.

Any buoyancy that Heatley's presence might have given the team evaporated after the first period of that night's game. The Thrashers held a 3–1 lead after 20 minutes, but Jeff O'Neill scored three times in the second period and Carolina held on for a 4–3 win — the Thrashers' ninth in a row without a victory. The Thrashers finally broke the streak by beating the Hurricanes 5–2 in Raleigh two days later. The win appeared to help steady the team. The playoffs were still within reach — but they had to keep winning. They won their second in a row, over Buffalo 4–1. J. P. Vigier was hit in the face with a stick in that game, breaking several bones that would eventually require several plates and metal screws to mend, but he nonetheless returned to the ice after the injury to score a goal. Still, the facial surgery meant another player lost to injury for the time being.

The day after the win over the Sabres, Heatley appeared on the ice at the Thrashers' practice facility without a red jersey. The longer practice went on, the more he went at it with teammates — no physical contact was spared. It was Heatley's birthday, January 21. He was making the final step towards returning to play. Afterwards, he took questions from reporters. "It feels good to be out there with the guys, finally," he said. "It was fun today." Heatley's return to the ice appeared to be imminent, still the team would announce no timetable.

"I think that will be the doctor's and trainer's call, and

[coach Bob Hartley's] call," Heatley said. "Right now, I'm just skating and doing what they're telling me. We'll see what happens." At one point during the practice Heatley had gotten tangled up with Patrik Stefan and he fell feet first into the boards. "That was probably a penalty on my part," Heatley said. "That was fine. It was pretty easy on my knee. It was more on my bottom."

Slava Kozlov was a member of the Detroit Red Wings in 1997 when they were struck by tragedy, but the circumstances were different from Dany Heatley's accident. Celebrating a Stanley Cup victory at a golf tournament, several players and the team masseur called for a limo to drive them home. The limo driver — later found to have marijuana in his system, although it was unknown whether he consumed it before driving — drove off the road, resulting in serious injuries for several of the passengers. That accident did not stir in Kozlov the same painful memories as Heatley's did. As horrific as it was, no one died.

In the fall of 1991, Kozlov's final season in Russia, he had just left behind his hometown team of Khimik Voskresensk and was playing 50 miles to the northwest with CSKA Moscow — the Central Sporting Club of Moscow, also known as the "Red Army." One year younger than Kozlov, Kirill Tarasov was also a Voskresensk native, and the two players knew each other from Khimik's youth programs, where Kozlov's father, Anatoli, was an instructor. Tarasov had been cut from Khimik, and Kozlov spoke with his coach at CSKA about arranging a tryout for his friend.

So with the 19-year-old Kozlov at the wheel, in the final days before Communism fell and the Soviet Union dissipated into history, the two embarked on the road from Voskresensk to Moscow. For anyone who has ridden on a Russian highway, the experience is one they will not soon forget. Drivers tailgate inches away from those in front of them — even if snow is falling or coating the road. An abrupt stop on whatever shoulder may exist is not uncommon; nor is it a surprise when the driver then puts his car in reverse. That day in 1991, Kozlov recalls driving behind a large truck for a long time.

"I don't remember the last 20 minutes before the accident," he said. He later learned from the police report that he'd hit a bus, which was making an illegal U-turn. In all probability, it happened when Kozlov switched lanes to get away from the truck and did not have time to stop before seeing the bus.

After the accident, Tarasov passed away in the hospital. Kozlov remained there for two months and needed another month of rehabilitation. He still bears the scars — physical and mental — of the ordeal. For several years following the accident, he suffered from depression. Selected 45th overall in 1990, before it was common for Russians to jump to the NHL, Kozlov decided it was finally time for him to leave home once he'd recovered. The Red Wings assistant general manager Nick Polano flew to Moscow, and through some colourful dealings, arranged for Kozlov to leave the country. As the story goes, a doctor declared that Kozlov had brain damage and needed care in the United States.

"It was just a way to get me out of the country," Kozlov said. "I was in the army. The Red Wings had to find a way to bring me here."

Upon arriving in Detroit, Kozlov found the transition was

not easy. For starters, he hardly spoke English. He said his attitude in those days was that if anyone wanted to speak with him, they had to speak Russian. "I was big-time depressed," he said. "I changed countries, lifestyles, language. The first year, I wanted to go home."

After that first season, Kozlov made his case to coach and general manager Bryan Murray, who wanted Kozlov to remain in the United States to train, learn English and continue to adjust to the culture. Kozlov, wanting to see his family and friends in Russia, prevailed. He spent most of the next season in the minors, but totaled 59 points in 45 games at Adirondack in the AHL. He remained depressed, but in retrospect speaks of the opportunity as a fruitful one for his career.

Kozlov played 77 games in the NHL the following season, and had the best regular season of his career. He credits Russian teammates Vladimir Konstantinov and Sergei Fedorov for helping him gradually pull out of the depression. "We spent lots of good times together," Kozlov said. "I felt lots of support from those guys." After the Red Wings' 1997 Stanley Cup victory, Konstantinov was severely injured when the limousine carrying the players crashed. The tough defenceman suffered severe brain damage that ended his career, and is now a shadow of his former self.

As much as seeing a close friend suffer was painful for him, Heatley's crash was overwhelmingly similar to Kozlov's Russian accident: two friends driving together, one at the wheel, the passenger ultimately dying. On September 30, 2003, a day the Thrashers were supposed to practice, players gathered at the team's practice facility in Duluth, Georgia. They made the decision not to skate that day. The decision also was made that the entire team would not address the media. Some players were emotional, and details of the accident were sketchy. Kozlov and Shawn McEachern, along with coach Bob Hartley, spoke to reporters in sombre tones. At the time, Kozlov was not prepared to discuss his own ordeal, in deference to his two teammates in the hospital.

A few days later, however, Kozlov was asked to share his experience in a more private way. He received a phone call from Murray Heatley, saying Dany wanted to see him. The previous season, the Thrashers had acquired centre Marc Savard from Calgary cheaply, as Savard had feuded with coach Greg Gilbert, who was fired shortly thereafter. When Hartley arrived, after constantly toying with line combinations, he put Heatley and Kozlov as wings on either side of Savard. The trio was as productive as any in the league. On the power play or at even strength, Heatley and Kozlov showed a chemistry: the power forward clearing space, while Kozlov, with his poise and artistry with the puck, set up Heatley for perfect opportunities that the big winger almost never missed. As Murray Heatley's call showed, that friendship and chemistry went beyond the ice.

Kozlov was not sure if the call for help from Heatley had come because of their friendship, or because of the knowledge that the Russian, too, had experienced something like what Heatley was going through. "I think both," Kozlov said. "I think he was kind of scared about what happened. I tried to talk to him. I had a hard time finding the right words.... From my own experience, at some point you have to stop all of the conversation about this accident. After Danny Snyder passed away, I told him, 'You're going to live with this for the rest of your life.'" Then Kozlov invoked a phrase used often at the time to describe the tragedy, and imparted some guidance he had received from Tarasov's mother, who supported him in the same way the Snyders have supported Heatley.

"I told him you have to play for the two Dannys now; how I'm playing. The rest of your life, you can't think about it every day." With Heatley set to return to play in late January 2004, Kozlov was among the most excited.

On January 22 against Colorado — Bob Hartley's former team — the Thrashers earned a costly 1-1 tie. They continued a three-game unbeaten streak, but that streak proved another pyrrhic victory. Physical rookie defenceman Garnet Exelby, who was chosen to play in the NHL's Young Stars game that year, suffered a hip contusion, and versatile forward Randy Robitaille sprained his knee. The injuries were getting to a point where they might be too much to overcome. That weekend, losses on back-to-back nights to the Islanders and Devils ended the winning streak and any momentum the Thrashers might have had to get back in the playoff race.

The Thrashers entered the following week missing nine skaters, including Heatley: defencemen Exelby, Tamer and Sutton; forwards Savard, Aubin, Vigier, Lindsay and Robitaille. The young franchise, with one of the league's lowest payrolls, did not have the organizational depth to compensate for such a decimation of the roster. The following week against the St. Louis Blues, defenceman Tomas Kloucek and Ivan Majesky, who was dressing, but still hobbled by a knee that was twice injured that season, combined to play a total of 4:13. That meant the foursome of Jean-Luc Grand-Pierre, Frantisek Kaberle, Daniel Tjarnqvist and Yannick Tremblay were forced to play an outlandish total of almost 30 minutes apiece.

At forward, minor leaguers like Daniel Corso, Zdenek Blatney and Brian Swanson were thrust into the lineup, and scoring leaders Shawn McEachern, Ilya Kovalchuk and Kozlov slumped. The overachieving of the beginning of the season had been strangled by a glut of injuries. Comparatively, the team they were trying to catch for first place in the division, the Tampa Bay Lightning, had lost just 14 man games to injury. By the end of February, Marc Savard had exceeded that total himself by five.

This was the setting one Tuesday afternoon after practice in Duluth, when reporters clustered around Dany Heatley to ask when he might be ready to return. His team needed him badly. He announced he would play the next night at Philips Arena against St. Louis — less than four months to the day since the accident. Heatley denied that the timing of his return had anything to do with the team's injury problems.

"It's nice to help, but this has no bearing on whether I was ready to play," he said. "This just happened to work out this way, and it'll be fun to get going again." Heatley's teammates were palpably excited about the prospect of his return. "He feels great, he looks good on the ice, and he's ready to help us," Kovalchuk said. "It's a tough time in the season right now. It's a key moment. If we can win some games, we're going to catch Tampa. I'm very happy for him. The first chance on the power play, we're going to have to give it to him."

The Fulton County District Attorney's office, which had yet to indict Heatley on any of the offenses with which he had been charged, issued a statement that day. "As the conditions of [Heatley's] bond allow for him to play and to travel for purposes of employment, this development is to be expected, and in no way reflects on the seriousness of the charges against him or the likelihood of any prosecution," it read in part. "We have nearly completed our thorough investigation of the complex matter at hand, and hope to be able to announce a charging decision soon." It was a line the office would continue to trot out, even as Heatley played in the World Championships in the Czech Republic in April and May, and then signed with a Swiss club once the NHL lockout commenced the following spring.

Heatley's highly anticipated return to the ice generated so much media interest that the Thrashers had to have special press conferences after the morning skate, and then again after the game for Heatley and coach Bob Hartley. In the morning, they used a room that normally acts as a player's lounge inside of Philips Arena, across the hallway from the locker room. After the game, they put a stage and chairs on the practice court used by the Atlanta Hawks. "It's opening night again for me," Heatley said that morning. Meanwhile, the organization vehemently denied that Heatley was returning too soon — his short rehab period seeming miraculous by any standard.

"I met with the doctors for the 17th time Saturday, and they assured me if we waited another week, month, three months, it wasn't changing anything," GM Don Waddell said. "He's 100 percent."

When it was announced Heatley was in the starting lineup, the crowd — which contained Heatley's parents — went wild. Before the game, Heatley had phoned the Snyders to ask them to attend the game, but they were on vacation in Las Vegas and told him they would come to a game soon. Following the Snyders' lead, fans brought signs with messages that embraced Heatley — "Welcome back Dany. We love you," and, "There goes my hero." Heatley had three excellent scoring chances during the game, but none of them got past Blues backup goalie Reinhard Divis, who was sharp — something that Heatley was not. The game finished a 1–1 tie and by overtime, Heatley was winded, but he reported no pain in his knee. His 22:55 of ice time was third-most among the team's forwards that night, as Hartley showed no shyness in using him.

"I felt pretty good," Heatley conceded after the game. "Overall, I was rusty here and there. My timing might have been off." About the way the crowd received him, Heatley said, "It was all excitement. It was a great feeling for me. They've supported me and [the team] through this whole thing."

Dany Heatley scored his first goal of the season his fourth game back, in a 5–4 loss at Boston. The game marked the team's seventh straight without a victory. The brief three-game unbeaten streak of the third week in January now started to look like an unrecognizable blip as the losses again snowballed. After trailing twice by a goal against Boston but rallying to tie, the Thrashers had their typical defensive lapse and gave up the winning goal with 93 seconds left in regulation. Despite his goal, Heatley did not appear overly thrilled.

"We can't worry about it too much," Heatley said of the loss. "We can worry about it, but it's over now. We have what, 27 games left now? And every game is a do-or-die game. We'll look at the video [today], but every game's got to have a win now. We've got to do it at this time of the year."

Three of those seven games without a win came before Heatley returned, but it was clear that he would not be the team's playoff saviour after all. For one, he could not play defence or goalie, positions where the Thrashers seemed unable to find any kind of stability. Secondly, it became obvious that he could not immediately find his scoring touch while beginning the season in the middle. The previous game, he'd had a golden opportunity at Tampa Bay and shot it right into Lightning goalie John Grahame; it was the kind of chance that would have resulted in an easy goal the previous season. "Terrible," was how Heatley described the shot, adding sarcastically that he was trying to place the puck "in the middle of his chest, of course."

After the Boston game, the Thrashers came home to lose to Philadelphia two nights later before the All-Star break mercifully gave them a few days off. One year earlier, Heatley had vaulted into stardom in the All-Star game. In 2004, he would sit at home while teammate Ilya Kovalchuk represented the team, as the league's highest vote-getter for the game. The Thrashers would resume the season after the break with a 12-day, seven-game road trip — their longest of the season — which swung through five of the six Canadian cities, all but Toronto. It began on February 10 in Calgary, Heatley's hometown.

Inauspiciously enough, the trip began with a photographer from the *Calgary Sun* being thrown out of the team's hotel for snapping a paparazzi-style sneak-attack picture of Heatley prior to a scheduled news conference the team had set up. The Snyders were in town for the game. They stayed with Heatley's parents and watched the game with them. It was the first time the Snyders would see Heatley play in person since his return, and they would travel the next day to Edmonton to see the team play again. Also at the game was Jeff Odgers, a well-liked veteran who had befriended Snyder and Heatley in previous seasons. Odgers, in retirement on his family's cattle ranch, drove the 10 hours from tiny Spy Hill, Saskatchewan, to see his former teammates.

Before the game at the Pengrowth Saddledome, Murray Heatley spoke for the first — and perhaps only — time publicly about his son's ordeal. "The Snyders have been absolutely wonderful," he told the *Atlanta Journal–Constitution*, breaking into tears. "It's unbelievable how they are. You'd like to think that you could handle it the same way, but you don't know if you could. Their Dan is gone, and here they are supporting our Dan every way they can. It's like they are part of our family now. They are incredible, forgiving people. It is all so tough. But the way the Snyders have been rekindles your faith in humanity. It really does. They have been so loving and caring." Five months after their son's death, the Snyders had become much more recognizable in their local community because of the media attention their saga had received in Canada. Yet Graham Snyder, picking up on a theme that would grow with time, would tell the Atlanta newspaper, "We're just normal people trying to do the right thing. . . . I know I've driven too fast in my lifetime and most other people have, too. I'm just lucky to be here to admit it. What happened to our son, and to Dany, was an accident."

After Calgary and Edmonton blew them out, the Thrashers ended their 10-game winless streak with a 4–1 win over

Vancouver. With that, they put behind them the quarter of a season that ultimately proved fatal to their playoff hopes. In 21 games starting on December 28 — the first game after Heatley's speech and the win over Tampa Bay — they had won just two.

February 23 fell on a Monday, two days after the team returned from the gruelling road trip. Dan Snyder would have been 26 that day. Dan Marr, who'd been instrumental in Snyder's rise to the NHL and had developed more of a close-ness with Snyder than he commonly did with players, called LuAnn Snyder that day to offer his condolences. LuAnn said that as each year's calendar passes, Dan's birthday would always rank among the most difficult for her family to get through. They would still celebrate the day but it would be without the one for whom they were celebrating. Recalling how her son was born at 8:30 a.m., LuAnn had told Dan she would call him at that time every year on his birthday. If he happened to be on a western road trip and it was 5:30 a.m. Pacific time, he would protest.

"I don't care," she would say. "This is the time it is here and that is when you were born." In 2004, for the first time, she had no phone call to make.

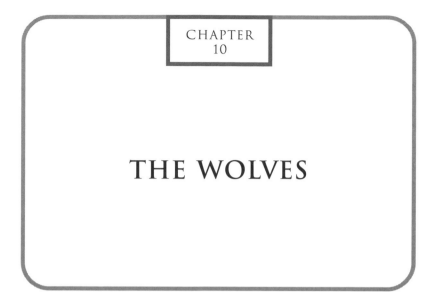

CHAPTER
10

THE WOLVES

Jarrod Skalde had just been sent down by the Dallas Stars from training camp to their AHL affiliate in Salt Lake City. Before arriving in Utah, the 32-year-old centre had returned to his offseason home in Orlando and packed up a U-Haul full of possessions. He gathered his wife, Erin, daughter, True, and infant son, Skate for the move to Utah for the coming season. The next day, they planned to stop in Atlanta, so Skalde phoned Dan Snyder to make plans to get together. The Braves were going to play the Chicago Cubs in the first round of the National League playoffs and Skalde called his sister-in-law who works for Turner, the parent company of the Braves, to get tickets. They had four. Snyder said he needed an extra. He, Dany Heatley, Skalde and some others planned on attending the game. Skalde got off the phone with Snyder at about 9:30 p.m.

that night. Snyder told him he and Heatley were just having a bite to eat and were heading home soon. They planned to meet at Turner Field the next night. It was September 29, 2003.

"He said, 'ok, cool, buddy, I'll talk to you and I'll see you in Atlanta,'" Skalde recalled. "Then I got a call at 5:30 a.m. from [Thrashers assistant equipment manager] Joey Guilmet. I drove to Atlanta and got to see them — Graham and LuAnn and Danny in the hospital. I was in there [Dan's room in the intensive care unit] with Jake. I got to say a few words, a few things like that. I was assuming he's going to be making a full recovery."

After Snyder died, so much publicity was paid to the public grief the Thrashers experienced. But Snyder — who had spent the overwhelming majority of his professional career in the minor leagues — had many close friends scattered throughout the hockey world. Some remained with the Chicago Wolves. Others, like Skalde, had bounced around, moving on to stints with the Philadelphia Flyers' organization, and a season in Switzerland before landing with the Stars before the 2003–04 season. Those close friends were every bit as grief-stricken as the Thrashers, but those who played with Snyder in Orlando and Chicago grieved in a much less public way. There were those like Skalde, Brad Tapper, Ben Simon and even tough guy Darcy Hordichuk, who, in Atlanta with the Florida Panthers for a pre-season game, visited Snyder at Grady Memorial Hospital and helped to wheel his former teammate from room to room. When Skalde arrived at Grady, he said the scene was surreal.

"I didn't want to impose," he said. "It was just bizarre. I don't know how to describe it. I saw a guy like Don Waddell and just gave him a hug. He had traded me a year before. In such a situation, you don't know how to act. I wanted to give the family some space. I was fortunate to spend some time there, with Graham, LuAnn and Jake. My wife was really close to Danny. She said it was tough to be around." The drive from Atlanta to Salt Lake took Skalde another three days. The Thrashers had provided members of the Snyder family with cell phones, and Skalde spent a good deal of time on the phone with Graham Snyder, receiving updates about Dan's condition. "It was comforting to get updates," Skalde said. "Then I remember getting that call from Jake late one afternoon that Danny had passed away."

Skalde left the Grizzlies for Elmira and the funeral, where he was one of the pallbearers. "The team was fairly good," Skalde said of his need to leave. "But they didn't have much say. This was something I had to do. The season started that weekend — like the whole hockey world. I just had to be around the family. People knew him. I had played five years ago [in Utah]. There were a lot of guys on the team I didn't know well, but this was a hockey tragedy. Everyone knew the situation. My teammates knew what I had to do." Skalde said Snyder's death and the ensuing funeral continued the unreal quality of those days. "I've been to funerals for elderly people, and some distant uncles and aunts," he said, "but nothing like this. You have memories that are so fresh. We were making plans an hour before he [got in the crash]. I've never had someone that close to me who passed away."

As time went on and he coped on a daily basis with Snyder's death, Skalde took strength from the outpouring of support at the funeral. "Obviously, I had moments where I'd sit there and cry," he said. "He was the guy you always called when you were doing something fun. He knew 10 or 15 guys like that. He was that type of guy. [But the funeral] motivated me so much. After seeing how the hockey world came around, it was unbelievable. I was so proud to be a hockey player. From across Canada and parts of the United States, it affected so many people — people who didn't know him. I thought, 'I'm in the best profession in the world: hockey.' People say it's just a sport, it's not life. When you see the funeral, it was all about hockey. That was the most important thing to me. It made me so proud to be associated with the people I was associated with."

Almost a year after his friend's death, Brad Tapper was blunt when he talked about how Snyder's death affected him. Nine months after signing Snyder, the Thrashers signed Tapper, a 6-foot, 180-pound right winger, out of the NCAA's Rensselaer Polytechnic Institute, and the pair played three seasons together in the IHL, AHL and NHL. They were two months apart in age and with Tapper making his offseason home in Toronto, lived 75 minutes apart. During the season, they shared a house together about 10 blocks from the Wrigleyville area of Chicago, near the Cubs' famed ballpark.

While their professional fortunes veered, their friendship did not. Snyder was assured a spot on the Thrashers' 2003–04 roster — with Bob Hartley favouring his grit — while Tapper struggled to score consistently and earned an early demotion during the 2003 training camp. That meant he was not around at the time of Heatley's car accident. On Saturday, October 4, five days after the incident, Thrashers GM Don Waddell travelled to Chicago and met with the Wolves the night of a game to provide the players with details on Snyder's condition.

Some players were new to the organization and did not know Snyder, so Tapper tried to be positive.

"He said everything's going to be fine," was Tapper's recollection of Waddell's message. Then, in regard to Snyder, Tapper told his teammates, "He's a tough guy. He's strong. He'll get through this." The next day, Snyder succumbed to septic shock. The news hit the media late on Sunday night, and then full throttle by Monday. "The landlord woke up my wife and me. We turned on the TV and it was devastating. I tried to get in touch with Jake right away."

In the weeks and months afterwards, Tapper's life spiraled downward. He had trouble coping with his friend's death. "After it happened, I didn't want to play hockey anymore," he said. "It was really tough. He's one of the strongest people I've ever known." Tapper attended Snyder's funeral in Elmira, but as a member of the Wolves — and not the Thrashers — he was not part of the funeral rite in the same way.

"There were maybe six or seven or us," he said. "Mike Weaver, Luke Sellars, a few other guys. . . . I was self-destructive in those days. I can't remember. The media attention was so much. You remember all the times you had together. You remember all the old times. It's tough when you lose a real good friend."

Tapper could not compartmentalize the loss. He talked about crying on the ice during games. His play suffered. He'd had 10 goals in 35 NHL games the previous season, but in 2003–04, just one in his first 20 games with Chicago in the AHL. "The year was shit from the beginning," Tapper said. "I didn't want to play. It was in my head all the time. My wife [Allison] really helped me out a lot. It's tough to cope with. It's just every night you're thinking about the fact he's not going to be around. It was devastating. I try to block it out so I can carry on."

But Snyder also served as an inspiration to Tapper, and kept him from perhaps his most destructive urges. "I wanted to quit," he said. "Snydes was never a quitter. We did a lot of stuff together all the time. If I ever saw him again and he saw that I quit, he'd kick me in the ass. He wouldn't let me do that." So Tapper soldiered on. The Thrashers traded him to Ottawa, where he played for the Senators' AHL affiliate in Binghamton, New York. Tapper was grateful for the fresh start and his play improved, but he was set back by a series of concussions. Gradually, he began to cope.

"My wife was great," he said. "My parents were good. My little brother, talking to Heater, it gives you a lot of strength."

Tapper said one of his turning points came in the summer of 2004. He attended the golf tournament Graham Snyder had organized to raise money for charities the family set up in Dan's name. As a minor-league teammate of Dan's, Tapper had befriended Snyder's family. He spoke with Jake Snyder, in particular, as often as was possible. That night after the golf outing, he and Jake stayed up late talking. Then Tapper decided to visit Snyder's grave. The cemetery is just a short distance from Graham and LuAnn's home. On a summer night, it might be a pleasant walk — a way to clear one's head. "It helped big time," Tapper said. "I went to the site myself and talked it over."

Preferring not to sign a minor-league contract with Ottawa in the summer of 2004, Tapper headed for Europe to play in Germany — even farther away from old memories, a place where he could look for a rebirth of his career. He was a long way from when he'd accepted the Thrashers' contract offer in

April 2000. Several months after signing his first NHL contract, Tapper had taken part in the organization's annual prospect camp, and was productive playing on a line with Heatley and Kovalchuk. Tapper bears no animus towards Heatley for what happened, saying, "Heater's a great guy." Tapper hopes a successful season in Germany could bring him back to the NHL.

A new city. Perhaps another new start.

Ben Simon brings two things with him wherever he plays. One is a black stick blade with Snyder's name stenciled in white letters. The other is a rectangular block of wood about four inches in length. Painted on one side is one of Snyder's favourite sayings, "Luck is what happens when preparation meets opportunity." On the other side, is a memento from Simon's first game with the Thrashers in 2003, a souvenir of an emotional reunion.

As hockey players, the scrappy Simon and Snyder were like bookends. In fact, the two played on a line together with both the Orlando Solar Bears and Chicago Wolves. Along with enforcer Darcy Hordichuk, the threesome hit everything that moved, helping lead the way to two minor-league championships.

"We had more bruises from hitting each other," Simon recalled fondly. Off the ice, Snyder and Simon also shared an affinity — for practical jokes. Leaning against a bin full of equipment outside the Wolves locker room in Chicago's All-State Arena, sporting four stitches over his left eye, Simon asks, "OK, you want stories? What kind? Off the wall stuff?" Simon is full of them. The first time he met Graham and Jake

Snyder, Simon started a food fight at a Super Bowl Party at a teammate's home. Snyder responded by throwing refrigerated plastic cups of chocolate pudding that exploded on the white walls. Another time, they were going to see the movie *Jackass* with Simon's wife, Beth, but planned to sneak a few beers into the movie theatre. The players left Beth Simon in the car and went into a grocery store. Snyder jumped into a grocery cart that Simon then flung into an elaborate display of what he remembers as Campbell soup cans. Simon ran out of the store, avoiding the wrath of store employees, but it was 30 minutes before a fuming Snyder returned from the manager's tongue-lashing.

But beneath the pranks was a strong friendship. At the conclusion of the 2002–03 season, Simon was a free agent and the Thrashers wanted to re-sign him. But it seemed his friend Snyder had locked up one of those spots for which Simon would have been best suited. A University of Notre Dame graduate, Simon made a business decision to sign with Nashville, thinking he would have a better chance to stick with the Predators in the NHL. On the morning of September 30, 2003, Simon was at training camp with Nashville in Orlando. When he woke up around 6 a.m., he checked his cell phone, whose ringer he had turned off the night before. He noticed he had four unanswered calls.

"I knew something was wrong," Simon said. Before he could check his voicemail, the phone rang. It was the Thrashers' Garnet Exelby, another former teammate with the Chicago Wolves. "He was pretty broken up. He told me what little information he knew. 'Snydes is pretty banged up but we don't know the extent.'" Three days earlier, Simon had played against the Thrashers in an exhibition game in Richmond,

Virginia. "Everything seemed fine," he said.

Nashville had visited Atlanta four days after the accident for both teams' final pre-season game. Simon felt the urge to go see Snyder in the hospital. "I called LuAnn and she told me, 'He's a battler. He'll make it through. Don't come to the hospital. Play the game. That's what he'd want,'" Simon said. After the return flight to Nashville, Simon was sent down to the Predators' AHL affiliate in Milwaukee. Along the way, he drove to Kalamazoo, Michigan, to pick up his pregnant wife before heading west to Milwaukee. At 2 a.m. on Monday, October 6, the phone call came from ex-Wolves' teammate Dallas Eakins.

"He said, 'We lost Snydes,'" Simon recalled. "It was less than 48 hours later [after he spoke to LuAnn]. It's hard to describe the loss of someone like that. He was my best friend in pro hockey. To have that void is unsettling, and it is today."

As was the case with Jarrod Skalde, Nashville and Milwaukee understood what Simon had to do as part of the hockey brotherhood. He and Beth headed east to Elmira instead of to Milwaukee. Several hours before the burial service, Simon visited the Snyders' home, where close friends and relatives had congregated. As the hour for the ceremony approached, Bob Hartley wanted to have a private meeting with his team. Simon stood awkwardly in the corner. In relaying the story, he pantomimed staring down at his feet, unsure of what to do. Seeing that Simon remained, Hartley called out to him, "You might not be a Thrasher, but you're still part of the family." Simon remains grateful for the gesture. "That awareness from Bob, he knew I was so overwhelmed," Simon said. "It meant a lot to me."

Simon returned to Milwaukee and played 18 games before fate took a painfully ironic twist. With Snyder absent, the

Thrashers' lineup missed the kind of agitator Hartley demands. At the same time, Nashville was shopping defenceman Tomas Kloucek, once a prospect prized for his size, but later damaged by shoulder and knee injuries. Waddell decided to take a chance. He packaged offensive-oriented defenceman Kirill Safronov, a former first-round pick, and diminutive-but-high-scoring forward Simon Gamache for Kloucek and Simon. Dan Marr from the Thrashers front office called LuAnn Snyder to tell her before even Simon was told the news, as Thrashers management figured LuAnn needed some good news. "I knew Dan would be happy," LuAnn said.

The same was true for Simon. "It was emotional," he said of returning to Atlanta. "I talked to LuAnn, and she said no one will ever know for sure, but she thought Dan was trying to get me back there any way." As Simon was getting dressed for his first game in his dressing room stall, Joey Guilmet walked over and placed a piece of tape on his locker. Guilmet had written a message on the tape. It said, "Play for Snydes and your family." Simon said he still gets the chills when he looks at it.

Back in Chicago, where he played during the NHL lockout, Simon showed off Snyder's stick blade and the block of wood with its dual remembrances. On one side was Snyder's favourite saying, on the other, the piece of tape. Then he brushed aside his jersey for that night, revealing one of the cards with Snyder's picture on it from the funeral. "My little buddy," he said. "That way I always have a piece of him wherever I go. . . .

"He made you want to be a better person," Simon said. "Dallas Eakins said it well, 'If you describe all the things you want to be in a person and all of the things you want to be in life and with that description, you come up with a picture of Dan Snyder.'"

Not long after he was called up to the Thrashers in January 2003, Dan Snyder had some explaining to do. Hartley had heard many versions of the infamous "circus story" involving Snyder, and he wanted to hear the definitive version — right from the horse's mouth.

Snyder had been banned from the Ringling Brothers and Barnum and Bailey Circus, which, coincidentally, was visiting Atlanta for most of the month, leaving the Thrashers, as always, on the road. But how does one get banned from the circus? There are many versions of the story, but it all started when Snyder was playing for the Chicago Wolves and the circus was visiting All-State Arena, the Wolves' home.

"Snydes decided that maybe he was going to have some fun and join the circus for a day," Wolves general manager Kevin Cheveldayoff said. The plan was that Snyder would run out of the Wolves' locker room wearing nothing but a towel, acting hurried as if he were late and needed to get into his costume, and that some unwitting circus hand would be complicit in handing Snyder something to wear to make the deception complete. But — like the elementary school prank that found Snyder the sole willing participant in mooning his audience — the joke soon was on Snyder.

"Someone pushed him out the door without a towel," Cheveldayoff said. "All of a sudden, he was locked out of the door buck naked." Well, maybe he was pushed out without a towel, or maybe he intentionally went out without a towel — but the locker room door was kept shut by a fellow prankster, unbeknownst to Snyder. "Well, then I had the manager of [the circus] on the phone," Cheveldayoff said. "We had a little chat. It turns out [Snyder] had to write a letter to [the circus] for the fact that some people saw him out there with no clothes on. . . . I still have a copy of the letter he sent." In the end, Snyder was able to convince circus officials that he was the victim of a prank. In return, they apologized to him. Many cite the story as typical Snyder — always coming out on top.

Unlike with the Thrashers, where he was a role player, Snyder was a catalyst and a leader on the Wolves. Those lessons he learned from Graham about looking the coach dead in the eye in critical game situations served him well. But so did his personality. The prankster, the joker who kept everyone loose — he also was the one who would look a teammate in the eye and tell him he was not pulling his weight.

"I think it was the fact that no matter what — whether it was the worst of times or the best, he always had a smile on his face," Cheveldayoff said. "You knew he was going to do something. Go out and play hard. Go out and pull a practical joke. He loosened the room up. Him and Benny Simon. I swear, we had to separate those two on game days. Those two, you never knew what they'd do in terms of practical jokes. Those are the memories you take with you. You win a championship and enjoy celebrating, but stories from inside the dressing room . . . . It makes you remember."

There was always something unique about Jarrod Skalde's relationship with Dan Snyder. Skalde was seven years older, and only knew Dan for two and a half years. But before he'd even met Snyder he had heard there was something special about him. During the 1999–2000 season, Snyder was a rookie in Orlando and Skalde was in his first stint with Utah, but already a 10-year pro. In December 1999, goalie Rick Tabaracci was traded from the Thrashers' organization to Colorado for Shean Donovan, and landed in Utah. An 11-year NHL veteran who had played with seven NHL teams, Tabaracci was in his final professional season.

"[Tabaracci] always talked about other players," Skalde said. "He said there's a kid there [in Orlando] named Dan Snyder. He's a phenomenal kid. For a 14-year veteran to say that with all of the players he's been around, this kid must be that good. It was the first time I heard of Snydes."

Skalde joined the Thrashers the following season. He played 19 games with them but spent 60 in Orlando as part of a Solar Bears club that won the Turner Cup. That is where he befriended Snyder. Skalde, the Niagara Falls, Ontario, native, echoed something LuAnn Snyder often says about what her son got from competing with older players so often when he was young. "I remember the exact night," Skalde said. "We went to Winnipeg on my first road trip. I sat down at a restaurant on a road trip with the older guys. I never felt he was a younger guy. He was just so mature. He's 22 and I'm 31. We rattled off every single Blue Jay we could imagine. This kid, he's got a better memory than I do. He knew hockey players from the '70s and '80s, and he was right there with me. Jesus Christ, this kid's supposed to be a kid. It was like talking to someone my age."

The godfather of Skalde's son Skate is Joey Guilmet, whom Skalde first met when he was playing for the San Diego Gulls in the IHL. Guilmet and Snyder also became close friends, and Skalde faced a difficult choice when he had to pick a godfather.

"I didn't want to burden Snydes at such a young age,"

Skalde said. "Obviously, he made the Thrashers and he was trying to stay there. I didn't want him to feel there was an obligation to be around my son or my family. I didn't think he'd take it as a burden, but I didn't want him to feel he had to do something special for my kid."

On Labour Day Weekend, 2003, Guilmet had been considering a trip from Atlanta down to Orlando, about an eight-hour drive, to visit Skalde and his godson. With training camp set to start in a few weeks, Guilmet was exhausted and was thinking of not going, until Snyder showed up at his house in his new truck and convinced Joey and his wife, Kim, to make the trip. To those there for the weekend, the trip made for an indelible memory.

"You just expect it with him," Skalde said. "I played in Switzerland the year before, and he told me, 'I'm going to visit you, but first I'm going to visit my new girlfriend in Los Angeles and my parents in Elmira. Then I'm coming to see you.' It was an important thing. It was right up there with going up to see his mom and dad in Elmira. It wasn't like, 'Oh, wow.' It was like, 'Yeah, he's coming. Of course, he is.' It wasn't out of ordinary."

Snyder was learning to play the guitar, taking lessons from some Atlanta musicians who were friends with Guilmet. Guilmet described Snyder as a natural. Skalde has a video of that weekend with Snyder playing guitar — one of the last recorded images of Snyder on tape. "They just pulled into the house," Skalde said. "We cracked a beer. My wife can't even watch it now. My wife grabbed the video and started filming. It's surreal to look at it now. There's about a three-minute clip of Danny playing guitar. One of the songs was Alice in Chains' 'Nothing.'" Ominously, the song's refrain is:

Well the nothin' song sticks to your mouth
Like peanut butter on the brain
Like peanut butter on the brain
Nothin' ever stays the same
Nothin', yeah nothin', nothin', nothin'

Skalde talks about the close bond between his family and Snyder. One summer, he and Snyder made a four-day trip to San Diego by themselves. Once Skalde's wife learned it was Snyder with whom he was making the trip, she did not bother him about it. Snyder was someone to be trusted. Snyder even made an impression on Skalde's young daughter, who was about six at the time of the crash. "My daughter called him Mr. Dan," Skalde said. "She prays to Mr. Dan sometimes. It's hard. I get sad sometimes, I get excited sometimes. He was so much fun all the time to be around."

CHAPTER 11

"HEAVEN IS A BETTER PLACE"

After the Thrashers snapped out of their 2-for-21 funk, they played well for the remainder of the season, going 12–8–2–2 in their final 24 games for 28 points. Had they played at that pace all season, they would have made the playoffs by five points. Instead, they missed by eight. By mid-February, they still had a chance to make the playoffs, but 12 wins would not cut it. They needed something more like 17 — an improbably difficult pace for an inconsistent team to sustain over 24 games.

To be sure, they staged more miraculous comebacks. Down by a goal at Ottawa on February 19, they tied the game with 10 seconds left in regulation, then won 3–2 in overtime. They sent a game to overtime on March 5 against Carolina with a goal by, of all players, Jean-Luc Grand-Pierre, with 13 seconds left in regulation. But they also threw away their share of points, as well. In Philadelphia on February 21, they trailed 3–0 after the first period and rallied to tie at 4–4. But with 61 seconds left in regulation Andy Sutton flung a broken stick at Simon Gagne, who was carrying the puck across the blue line on a harmless 2-on-2. Gagne was awarded a penalty shot, scored, and the Thrashers lost in regulation. Exasperated Thrashers Pasi Nurminen, Ilya Kovalchuk and Marc Savard broke their sticks in anger after the game and cursed at the officials. At Boston on March 6, the team led 2–1 with five minutes left in regulation, but gave up a power-play goal on a questionable penalty call and finished with a tie. Three days later, they lost 2–0 to the Rangers, who had just traded nine players — Brian Leetch among them — before the trading deadline expired, leaving the team virtually bereft of NHL talent save Jaromir Jagr, Mike Dunham and Bobby Holik, the two goal-scorers that night.

Another notorious game came March 17 against Buffalo. The Thrashers led 3–1 late into the third period, when enforcer Francis Lessard jumped Buffalo's Andrew Peters before a face-off in one of those unwritten hockey rituals in which both combatants agree to fight as soon as the linesman drops the puck. But Peters knelt to the ice and covered up against the blows; in hockey parlance, he turtled. The ploy worked. Lessard received seven minutes in penalties, as Peters received none, and Adam Mair, Dan Snyder's junior teammate in Owen Sound, took advantage of exhausted penalty killers and made it 3–2 with 7:37 left. Jochen Hecht tied it 1:24 later at even strength, then Derek Roy won it 15 seconds into overtime on a long shot that Nurminen never should have missed.

One of the bright spots at the end of the season was that the team finally called up highly touted goalie prospect Kari Lehtonen from the Chicago Wolves. Lehtonen had a groin strain that had prevented a call-up early in the Thrashers' swoon, when GM Don Waddell had hoped the young Finn might give the team some life. Lehtonen won all four of his starts, including the season finale at Tampa Bay — a bittersweet indication of what might have been. Waddell would later hint that the team's impending ownership change had tied his hands in terms of being able to add salary and acquire some available forwards like the Chicago Blackhawks' Steve Sullivan (who went to Nashville) and Alexei Zhamnov (who went to Philadelphia).

"Because of our situation, there were things we could and could not do economically," Waddell conceded after the season. As good as Lehtonen was over the final two weeks, coach Bob Hartley saved the final home start of the season for Nurminen, who received the team's player's player award.

In that final home game on April 2, the Snyders returned to Atlanta for an on-ice ceremony honouring their son. The Thrashers had created the Dan Snyder Memorial Trophy, which would be given each year to the team's unsung hero. Graham, LuAnn, Erika, Jake and his girlfriend Dawn Moore walked onto a red carpet on the ice where team captain Shawn McEachern skated over and presented them with Dan's jersey, which Joey Guilmet had faithfully hung in Snyder's locker stall every game. The players had autographed the jersey, and LuAnn had to wipe away a tear as McEachern handed it to her. "It's a real honour," Graham Snyder said that night. "It's something Dan would've appreciated because he was always kind of an unsung player."

The inaugural award went to rookie defenceman Garnet Exelby. Exelby and Snyder were teammates for two seasons with the Chicago Wolves. In Chicago, Exelby, a Saskatchewan native more than three years younger than Snyder, sat in the same corner of the dressing room as Snyder. He recalled Snyder's comic accents and impressions. "We'd all not like to have the award, but it's something I'll cherish forever," Exelby said at the time. With the perspective of time, he added, "I couldn't pick a better award to win, realistically. I'm very proud of that award and proud of having Dan's name on it. . . . The commitment and emotion that he put into the game, and love he put into the game. . . . I'd love to be associated any way I could with him."

With a $25,000 donation, the Snyders created the Dan Snyder Neuro-Trauma Fund at Emory University Hospital. The Thrashers pledged for the first five years of its existence to donate $15,000 to that fund in the name of the player who wins the award. One year after Dan's death, the fund, dedicated to teaching, research and clinical care in neuro-trauma, had also received $25,000 in private donations.

The Kingston, Ontario-based rock band the Tragically Hip might play small clubs in the United States, and their songs might receive little if any airtime on mainstream American radio, but their popularity in Canada might be unsurpassed at the moment. The group sells out large venues in Toronto, like the Air Canada Centre, in a matter of hours for multiple shows. For his showmanship and the intellectual quality of the lyrics he writes, lead singer Gord Downie has been described by critics as a composite of the Rolling Stones' Mick Jagger and REM's Michael Stipe. The band members are big hockey fans, and incorporate that passion into some of their music. One famous song is about legendary Toronto Maple Leaf Bill Barilko, whose goal in Game 5 of the 1951 Stanley Cup finals proved the series-clincher. That summer Barilko embarked on a plane for a fishing trip and was never seen again. His remains and the wreckage of the plane were found in 1962, which, coincidentally, was the first time the Leafs had won the Cup since his legendary goal.

About two months before the Tragically Hip released their album, *In Between Evolution* on July 12, 2004, the band's manager phoned Jake Snyder. The band wanted Jake to know that it had written a song about Dan. Jake was moved, to say the least.

"It's hard to describe the feeling," he said. "A band so popular, it was a pretty big honour. Dan was a big fan and I've grown up with them since I was a kid. I was touched by the gesture." Not the least of it was that Jake plays in a band of his own — Funky Rudy — that covers the band's songs.

At the time of the accident, the Hip were in Whistler, British Columbia, recording the album. They were riveted by news reports in part because of a personal connection they felt to the events. They had met Dany Heatley backstage one night after a show in Atlanta. Snyder had been with Heatley that night, but he did not go backstage to meet the band.

"I was talking to Dany in Calgary a month or so ago," Downie said in September 2004. "Dany said it was a real regret of his that we couldn't have all met. That it would've been big for Dan, too."

The title of the song is "Heaven Is a Better Place Today."

Downie said he was inspired by Snyder's everyman quality, by the dignity his family displayed in the midst of tragedy, and by its ability to forgive Heatley. "Dan Snyder was the guy we all can relate to," Downie said. "The guy who worked hard, and through sheer grit and determination made the team. . . . There was a lot of language floating around that tragedy — through the vigil and through his funeral and days after — that had a lot of eloquence. You feel compelled to say something. Words become very important. You're at a loss for them most of the time. Really, I was trying to piece together a lot of those things with the song . . . I wanted it to be hopeful for everyone involved."

> Here's a glue guy a performance god
> a makeshift shrine newly lain sod
> hardly even trying gives the nod
> I sure hope I'm not the type to dwell
> hope I'm a fast healer fast as hell
> heaven is a better place today because of this
> but the world is just not the same
> if and when you get into the endzone
> act like you've been there a thousand times before
> don't blame don't say people lose people all the time
>   anymore.
>
> A toonie to the busker and a husky 'keep it comin' under
>   my breath
> but then said, 'though, if you wouldn't mind,
> less crying and more trying more trying and less crying'
> I'm not the type to dwell
> I'm a fast healer fast as hell

heaven is a better place today because of this
but the world is just not the same
oh if and — if and when you get into the endzone
act like you've been there a thousand times before
don't blame and don't say people lose people all the time
   anymore.

If and when you get into that endzone
act like you've been there a thousand times before
don't change but don't say people lose people all the time
   anymore

It's just not the same because of this
it's not the same

Five years younger than Dan, Erika Snyder did not relate to her brother through the sport that was his vocation. As a child, she was always being dragged to his hockey games, but LuAnn Snyder said Dan had a special affection for his sister from the time they were small. LuAnn cited an instance when Erika was a toddler and wandered out of the house without anyone's knowledge. She described the worried state of Dan, who was only five or six at the time, and how he was the one who tracked down Erika. But as with Dan's relationship with Jake, Erika endured her years of being teased and fighting with Dan.

It was not until she grew older that she came to relate to Dan through music. Like her brother, Erika Snyder is a self-taught guitar player. Dan would relay stories to his sister about the Atlanta musician from whom he was taking lessons. "'You will not believe this guy. He calls himself Evil Jimmy. He lets me wail on it.' He thought it was so funny," she said. They shared a common interest in bands like the Lassue Yous, Billy Talent, Pearl Jam, Metallica and the Tragically Hip. So, to this day, one of Erika's most prized possessions is her brother's guitar. When the family first took hold of Dan's possessions after he died and received his guitar, they thought someone had made a mistake. Dan's guitar had had a rounded back. This one was different. Later, it was explained to them that, amid some horsing around during Snyder's stay with Heatley — what Erika jokingly referred to as "being idiots" — Heatley had accidently broken that guitar and bought Snyder a new one. (Jake said his brother had a Pete Townshend–like zeal for breaking guitars.)

Erika was travelling when Jake received the call from The Hip about the song written in Dan's honour. Erika felt the same way as Jake did about the gesture, referring to the band as a "Canadian institution."

"When we saw them play it live, we were sitting in the third row," she said. "They could see us and they waved at us. They said, 'This is for Jake.' It was cool." More than any other member of the immediate family, Erika has shied away from the media spotlight. Her mother sometimes refers to her as "the forgotten one in all of this," but Erika does not feel that way. She was home when the phone would ring 10 times with reporters calling about some new development in Heatley's case and, seeing her father having to deal with it, felt fortunate to be spared. She does not feel forgotten because within her family, she knows her suffering has been equally appreciated.

Only with the perspective of time can she appreciate what she went through. She'd formed a close friendship with Dan's girlfriend, Lisa Rotondi, and has visited Rotondi in Los Angeles. "I didn't really remember much about what happened afterwards," Erika said. "People tell me stuff. I remember everything from the hospital, being there when he died. There was so much going on, so many people. I was a little bit in shock. . . . Three weeks after the funeral, I went and stayed with [Rotondi] for a week. At the time I was thinking I was OK. We talked a lot. Six months later, I went again and we talked about when I came for the first time. I realized, 'Oh, my God, I was a complete basket case.' I would cry spontaneously. It's funny how you deal with things without processing them."

Erika Snyder visits Lisa Rotondi every few months. Rotondi calls Erika "her sister for life." An actress from Minnesota who has gotten roles in television shows like *Friends*, CSI *Miami*, CSI, NYPD *Blue*, the HBO series *The Mind of the Married Man* and the film *The Mating Habits of the Earthbound Human*, Rotondi met Dan at a New Year's Eve party in 2002, through the wife of Wolves teammate Dallas Eakins, who also is an actress. Rotondi and Snyder dated on and off for the next nine months with her in Los Angeles and him in Chicago and Atlanta. During the summer of 2003, she spent a week getting to know his family in Elmira.

The relationship might have been short, but it was intense. Rotondi said they spoke almost daily for hours on the phone. The relationship was enough to inspire Rotondi to loosely base a screenplay of a romantic comedy on their lives. Rotondi has written a script for the film, which she has dubbed *Hat Trick*, and has fully funded. The film was to start shooting two years to the date after Snyder died: October 5, 2005. After trying to go through a major studio, she switched to the independent route and has raised $75,000, while needing an additional $200,000.

"The movie is this," Rotondi said. "A woman makes a list for her perfect man, which is the opposite of her father, who is overbearing and passive-aggressive. She's a healer living in Venice, California. She uses crystals, does chants, and meditates. The love of her life is a yoga instructor to the movie stars. On page four [of the script], he dumps her when she thinks he's about to propose. It cuts to three months later. She's in Venice making pathetic attempts to get her boyfriend back. Her whole family is coming to visit her — her suicidal brother who wants to be Jamaican, her father who mixes his metaphors, her mother. Cut to page six. She's at yoga still trying to get [her ex-boyfriend] Matt back, and her friend who is married to a minor-league hockey player takes her to a game. She's mortified by the violence. She keeps telling someone to stop it. Then she meets this guy Joe Bender, No. 19 [Snyder's number in Chicago]. He's a fighter. He's fought and worked his way up, and now he's going to the NHL. He brawls and scores a couple of goals. He trips over a rut in the ice and pulls his groin — that was Dan's idea, the groin thing.

"At the end of the game, they go to this bar, and she's still pining over Matt. She tells Joe, 'I'm a healer. I can fix your groin.' He thinks she's trying to get him in the sack. He makes fun of her, but in a light way. So they get together, obviously, in sort of a hilarious way. The family's there for the second act. All hell breaks loose." In short, boy loses girl, boy wins girl back. "In the end, Jessie [the main character] is at a hockey game, yelling, 'Kill the mother [expletive]!'"

Since Snyder's death, Rotondi has become even more

determined to get the film made. She has promised Snyder's friends — Dallas Eakins, Jarrod Skalde, Ben Simon, Brad Tapper, Dany Heatley — bit parts in the film. The fictitious team's name is the Monrovia Night Owls, and the fans yell "Whooo!" when they score. "I am 100 percent going to play the part," Rotondi said. "It's the only story I ever have with him. . . . [Snyder's death] was the most life-changing event in my life. I can't say enough about the guy."

The Thrashers' Dan Snyder Memorial Trophy was just one example of the ways in which the Snyders got involved in charity work after Dan's death. Because of the many humanitarian causes he undertook, the Snyders say they felt obligated to continue on with that kind of work in his name. In less than a year after his death, Dan had awards created in his honour by Owen Sound, the Ontario Hockey League, the Chicago Wolves and the Thrashers.

Courtney Mahoney, the Chicago Wolves director of community relations and game operations, said she was not so high on Snyder when she first met him. He had come from Orlando — the team that had defeated Chicago for the IHL championship the previous season — and she did not forget his notoriously abrasive playing style. But during a photo shoot for the team's media guide that pre-season, he approached her about doing work in the community. "He wasn't my favourite," Mahoney said. "But he came up to me and said, 'Whatever you need me to do, I'm interested. I don't want to be sitting around and doing nothing.' I had never had a player volunteer to do community stuff. He helped out quite a lot. He rear-ended me once when I didn't know him as well. I thought, 'This guy's going to be a beauty.' We were leaving a library [after conducting a session of the Wolves' "Read to Succeed" program]. Usually, you did two a day. We were down [at the south end of Chicago], going from one to another. I checked back to make sure he was following me. All of a sudden, I come to a stoplight and he plows into me. Fortunately, I had no damage, but he had a little Jeep Wrangler that was worse than mine. He was dying. He was embarrassed. He was looking at his phone or something. It's definitely one of my great memories of him."

Mahoney said Snyder brought zeal to his charity work. "Whenever we did hospital visits — there are so many guys who go through the routine, but I think he enjoyed it — he had a presence about him, the kids gravitated to him, that look with the crazy hair. When you have a guy like that, the kids love it." She mentioned another Wolves' charity event, "Get Fed By the Wolves," in which the players act as waiters and charity items are auctioned off. "The two of them [Snyder and Ben Simon] were getting $800 donated for a T-shirt. They would goof around and sacrifice themselves. We did the auction at Max and Erma's one year and they covered themselves with stuff at the sundae bar. Needless to say, we weren't invited back, but we raised over $10,000. I think he just thought it was funny. Their shirts went for more than anybody else's. Dan did a chicken dance up there. You could be embarrassed if he was up there."

In the two seasons immediately following Snyder's death, Mahoney said he left a legacy that his teammates were eager to carry on. "We certainly always had great guys throughout our tenure, but [Snyder] was the first time we had someone offer and follow through. Now it's such a legacy, ever since that and we named the award after him. Usually you have your one guy to nominate to the league, but now guys are anxious to be a part of it. They've taken a following to what he's done. 'What do you need me to do? I'm going to step up in Dan's footsteps.' It continues to pass."

So not just Snyder's teammates, but his family felt the need to carry on that legacy, as well. There also would be scholarships, helped by an NHLPA-funded auction, to four university-bound athletes in southern Ontario. Thanks to the proceeds from the auction, game-worn jerseys from the December 31, 2003 game between the Thrashers and Detroit Red Wings, the fund is now self-sustaining. But what is most important to the Snyders is that an ice rink and indoor sports complex ultimately is built in Elmira bearing Dan's name.

Before Dan died, Woolwich Township commissioned a study as to the feasibility of replacing Elmira's old rink — the one where Dan played his minor and junior hockey with Elmira's Sugar Kings, before moving on to Owen Sound. Dan was simply irate when his parents explained to him that the township's fiscally conservative leaders did not want to go into debt to build a new facility, projecting in a study that they would not be able to afford a new one for 13 years. Dan pledged to do his best with contacts in the NHL to raise money to help build a rink sooner.

After Dan died, the idea that such an arena be constructed — a project which the Snyders fervently supported before knowing how their son felt — took on an even greater urgency. They still raise money by selling No. 37 pins — the idea for which came from the Thrashers front office as a way for employees to honour Dan; players wore a patch with his number on their uniforms at games, but other employees, who did not wear uniforms to work, wanted to show their public support. At youth tournaments like the one in Blenheim where Graham spoke in December 2004, young players and coaches gobble them up in large numbers.

The plans for the arena the Snyders, along with the community, have conceived would cost $10 to $15 million to put into action. They envision one-third coming from local funds, one-third coming from provincial or federal funds and one-third coming from the community, a portion of which would come from the Dan Snyder Memorial Fund. Approximately one year after Dan's death, the memorial fund — which is overseen by a board including Snyder's former agent Don Reynolds, an Elmira banker and other professionals — held $250,000.

The largest single fundraiser is the golf tournament which the Snyders expect to hold each July. The tournament became such a logistical load that Graham Snyder resigned his job as general manager of Elmira's Junior B team to focus on it.

"When the [2003–04] season was over, I didn't have the time or energy to do the general manager's job in the proper way," Graham said. "I had to work on the golf tournament. I didn't have time to devote. I preferred to step down."

The first annual golf tournament in Dan Snyder's honour was scheduled for Tuesday, July 13, 2004. Back in Atlanta, the Fulton County grand jury — the body that decides whether the prosecutor has enough evidence to support a charge and warrant an indictment, which then leads to a trial — met only on Tuesdays and Fridays. For weeks, rumours swirled that Heatley's indictment was imminent. The prosecution had kept the Snyders abreast of developments, so the family waited tensely and quietly, dreading what might come. Throughout the legal proceedings, the Snyders made a pact that none of the news would ever leave the family and stuck to it. They knew the expected day of the indictment — and had to plead with prosecutors not to ruin the golf tournament by indicting Heatley before it, or on the same day.

The tournament proved to be festive, with professional hockey players and other celebrities turning out to support it. Dany Heatley attended, and he, his parents and his brother Mark stayed with the Snyders. Many members of the Thrashers were also there, with the tournament's winning foursome being Marc Savard, Andy Sutton, Garnet Exelby and Chris Tamer. TSN's Bob MacKenzie acted as master of ceremonies. Don Cherry, who once alluded to having Dan Snyder's picture on his dresser, left a message on the Snyders' answering machine apologizing for not being able to attend. On the course, the participants feasted on summer sausage, a local specialty. At the tournament's awards ceremony, the winners were presented with red and pale-blue blazers, a spoof of the Master's tradition of the green jacket, and a tribute to Dan's predilection for goofy clothes.

Two members of the Tragically Hip, Paul Langlois and Gord Sinclair, took part in the golf tournament, as well. That night, the festivities continued, and the band members joined in, with Langlois playing Dan's guitar and later signing it. Jake, the front man of his own band, got involved and sang along with the band whose songs he covers. As Jake and the members of the Hip played that night before some of the young people of Elmira, Dany Heatley got to enjoy a moment of anonymity. "He was just a person there," LuAnn would say. The day's events acted as a salve for the Snyders on their journey of healing.

Three days later, that process would take a step backwards.

CHAPTER 12

CARDS AND LETTERS

Dan Snyder's room is in the basement of the Snyders' 100-year-old home. The room is small, and has but a single window, insufficient for allowing much light — the better for sleeping late. It's cool in the summertime. For all these reasons, LuAnn dubbed it "the cave." As a teenager, Dan painted the walls the sky blue of his favourite team, the Quebec Nordiques. His father used an overhead projector to help trace the logo. Dan's personal effects are everywhere — on the bed, on the floor, in the closet. Jerseys that signal some kind of personal milestone hang in the closet: Thrashers home and away jerseys bearing the No. 99, the year he signed; Chicago Wolves and Orlando Solar Bears jerseys from their championship seasons; an Owen Sound Platers jersey; an Elmira Sugar Kings jersey.

Inside the closet are two shopping bags filled with cards

and letters. One holds get-well cards the Snyders have never gone through. The other, weighing 10 or 15 pounds, is a bag filled with condolences, more than 2,000 in all. About two days after Dan died, the cards started coming in a deluge. The mailman had to come twice a day just to keep up with the workload. One is addressed simply to "Mr. + Mrs. Snyder (Dan's parents) Elmira, Ontario," without a postal code or street address. It arrived without a problem. People sent pictures of Dan when he made appearances at schools and hospitals. Some sent handwritten letters six, eight or 10 pages in length.

The letters come from a myriad of sources: former teammates at every level; neighbours; relatives; Lou Lamiorello; the New York Islanders booster club; fans; the Calgary Buffaloes, Dany Heatley's midget team; complete strangers from across Canada and the United States. The sentiments they express are enough to renew one's faith in humanity. More than a year and a half after Dan's death, the letters still come.

11/3/03

Isn't it wild how life doesn't prepare us for the unexpected — even those of us that are a bit more "go-with-the-flow" types can't help but be thrown by some of the terrible unexpected events as they unfold around us. I wish you peace as you wrestle with those mountain size questions and emotions that are yours to look at now.

Strength from family and friends is an enormous and absolutely great thing to have happen

around you and, as a friend, albeit one at a bit of a distance over the past some time, I would like you to know that I hope the best for you while you deal with some of the worst that can happen to you.
    — Bob Martin

❋

We cannot begin to tell you how deeply saddened we are by your great loss of a dear son and brother, Dan. Our prayer for you is comfort, strength, and courage to face each new day. It is only through faith that you can let Dan go. In time, may your tears of sadness be replaced with tears of joy as you remember what Dan was all about — his determination and work ethic to let nothing get in his way of fulfilling his lifelong dreams. What an inspiration and message to be shared with other teens. He experienced so much in such a short 25 years.

Death may be the end of a lifetime but never of a relationship as a son and brother. That can never be taken away from you. Hold on tight to those memories as you forgive in order to move forward in your grief journey. May you continue to be a blessing to others as you have been in the past, and may you feel the love and support and blessings of a community of family and friends.

> *Lord, help us through our grief and loss —*
> *Through valleys deep when Dan is gone;*
> *Then heal our hearts, renew our joy,*
> *Grant us the strength to carry on.*

With love and friendship and appreciation for all
that you do in helping others,
      — Elder and May June

When the Thrashers played their first exhibition game after the accident on October 1, Mark Holland knew plenty of fans would be wearing Dany Heatley paraphernalia — after all, it was sold in abundance after Heatley's 2003 All-Star performance. What was harder to obtain were shirts and hats with Dan Snyder's name or number on them, as he had only played 36 games in the NHL the previous season. A native Atlantan, Holland, 22 at the time of the accident, is a season-ticket holder, but the connection he felt towards the team transcended that of the rooting interest of most fans.

During his freshman year at Indiana University in fall 1999, Holland contracted strep throat. Treatments for the infection were unsuccessful. He remained bedridden. Colds and flus persisted to the point where doctors thought he might have had leukemia. His illnesses caused him to withdraw from school. Eventually, doctors determined that Holland had mononucleosis, and prescribed the steroid prednisone, which cured him for the time. Two years later, he had a relapse. Again he was bedridden, and again he had to withdraw from Indiana.

"At that point, I didn't want to live anymore," he said. "I thought I would never get better . . . I just wanted to die. I was bedridden and I was losing the best years of my life."

During his recuperation in Atlanta, Holland found something to look forward to: the Atlanta Thrashers. Bad as they were in 2001–02 — and they were the worst team in the NHL

— Holland would attend every practice. One of the benefits for hockey fans in a nontraditional market like Atlanta is that the team has to earn the affection of its fans. They do not just automatically show up like Toronto Maple Leafs fans do, or New York Yankees fans do. So the Thrashers open all of their practices at IceForum in Duluth to fans. As players walk the short distance from the ice to the double doors that lead to the dressing room, fans line up for autographs. Because they were similar in age, Brad Tapper and Darcy Hordichuk became two of Holland's favourites that year.

When Holland learned of the life-threatening nature of Snyder's injuries, his interest was more than casual. "It was like the Thrashers became family to me," he said. "They meant that much. So when Dan and Dany went down, it was like someone in my family went down." Holland decided to act that night after the Thrashers beat Florida. He designed a simple T-shirt with Snyder's name and number on the back and the words "In Our Hearts" on the front, and a scan of an autograph Holland had received from him. Holland posted the design on one of the Thrashers' fan Web sites and decided to sell the shirts for $30, with the proceeds going to the Thrashers Foundation, a series of children's charities that the team designates. He purposely avoided using the team's name or logos to avoid trademark issues.

As orders for the shirts grew each day, he decided to seek Don Waddell's permission. He sent the e-mail on Saturday, October 4. Snyder died the next day. At that point, Holland wondered if it was appropriate to continue his enterprise. His parents counselled him to stop. Waddell's permission became that much more urgent to him. On the Monday before Waddell was to be the face of the organization at a news conference on

Snyder's passing, the general manager granted Holland his permission. "God bless Don Waddell," Holland said. "He e-mailed me Monday morning. He said, 'I know your intentions are good. Please continue.'"

Holland changed the shirts to read, "In Our Hearts Forever." Orders kept coming in but to be able to fill the orders in time for that Thursday's opener, he placed a deadline of Monday for orders. Holland raised more than $5,000 from the shirts. His father had joked with him during the process that if Mark raised $5,000, he would pay for Mark to fly to Elmira and personally present the check. His father also topped off the donation so that the check would be for a clean $6,000. After Dan's death, the Snyders had designated two charities for people to donate to: Woolwich Minor Hockey and Emory University's Neurosurgery Department. Holland decided he wanted the money to benefit the children of Elmira.

Without touching any of the money from the proceeds, his father flew Mark to Elmira to present the donation. To this day, he maintains a relationship with LuAnn, occasionally e-mailing and phoning. Holland's story is but one example of the outpouring of support the Snyders have received in the death of their son and brother.

Dear LuAnn,
My thoughts are with you. You have been such a
supportive and enthusiastic mom. I'll miss your
terrific stories of Dan's latest challenges and suc-
cesses. Dan was an exceptional young man with
an exceptional family. I'm so sorry for your loss. At

the funeral, I got a picture of Dan's character which looked similar to yours. May the love, strength and determination you shared, help to carry you through the days ahead.
With fondest regards.
— Marilyn

✳

My family and I want you to know how sorry we are to hear about your Dan. You must have been very proud of him. My seven-year-old son started hockey after seeing him play — he was a hero to many little boys. Again, we are so, so sorry for your loss.
Peace be with you,
— Stacey Allen

✳

I love Dan Snyder. I do play hockey. Your son was the best hockey player.
— From Cullen

✳

To the parents of Dan Snyder,
Please accept my most heartfelt sympathy and prayers with Dan's passing. He meant a great deal to my family and touched us in ways that I'd like to share with you, not the least is that my daughter's cat is named Snyder after Dan.
My son died when he was 16 in Illinois and was a huge hockey fan. My daughter Jaclyn's best

friend is Karlie Reif, and our pastor, who helped us so much, was her father Joel Reif. Joel's son Clint played hockey until he had too many concussions and then became assistant equipment manager for the Solar Bears after the whole family moved to Florida.

Dan and my John bore big physical resemblances and had such wonderful free spirits and such kindness.

Jackie, who is now 20, moved to Florida to be with Karlie Reif in October, three years ago, the year Dan was a starter with the Solar Bears. She saw every home game and I planned my Florida vacations around their schedule.

His death leaves an emptiness. Please know what joy his friendship and spirit brought to my daughter and, thus, myself.

Your family is in my prayers. It is with great understanding that I try to share your overwhelming grief.

With sympathy to you all,
— Loral Hahn and Jaclyn Howard

✳

Danny Boy —
You will skate with us forever. You are the best.

Watch over us and guide us in getting that puck in the net.
— The Trumpolt Family
Clay, Nancy and Rich # 7

✳

There are no words that can ease your pain now, but please know that your "hockey family" is praying for you. While we may all cheer for different teams during the season, the sadness of your loss is felt by all NHL fans.
God Bless
— Donna and Michael Sweet, Gahanna, Ohio

Among the most unusual pieces of mail the Snyders received was a cardboard cylinder several feet long from a New York University art student. Xenia Rybak was a 21-year-old senior at the time of Dan's death who had grown up with hockey "intertwined totally in my life," as she put it. Her older brother Mark played, and the family lived not far from the New Jersey Devils' practice facility in West Orange, New Jersey. "My brother was a supporter when Wayne Gretzky called them a Mickey Mouse organization," Rybak said. The brother and sister and their friends followed the organization from its embarrassing beginnings to its rise to the top of the NHL.

Rybak had created at least one piece of hockey-inspired artwork before the accident, but when she learned of Snyder's passing she felt compelled to make another. "Having an older brother, they're so close to my age, Dan and Dany," Rybak said. "I looked at Dany Heatley and I was like, 'His life is forever changed.' I looked at Dan and thought about how people die every day in car accidents. But it's a face to a name. It hit a chord with me. I don't know why it hit me so hard, but it did."

For three weeks, she compiled headshots of every player in the NHL at the time of Snyder's death. Even as a hockey fan, Rybak had not heard of Snyder before the accident — something she feels guilty about. She kept thinking of Heatley's toothless grin during the previous season's All-Star Game, and how his life would never be the same. She alphabetized the nearly 700 player photos, by team and by player, and arranged them in rows: ten across and thirty-five down. Each photo is a few inches long. At eye level sits Snyder's photo, four times larger than the others. When she was finished, she mailed the long sheath of photos to the Snyders in the cardboard cylinder.

"What I wanted to do was to convey that it was taller than a standard person, and he's on your eye level and you're overwhelmed by it," Rybak said. "I switched the titles a couple of times. Only my professor knew why the one person was in the middle. [Jaromir] Jagr was the last person, and he was traded by the time I was done. It's such a temporary piece, but it didn't bother me at all. The piece was created in that moment in time forever. That's how the NHL was structured."

In addition to being so close in age to Heatley and Snyder, Rybak said she was touched by the Snyders' act of forgiveness. She included those sentiments in a letter she enclosed to the Snyders when she sent them the work. "It's one thing for parents and siblings to have forgiveness but they had it so quickly for Dany," she said. "I wrote that in the letter. I don't even remember what I wrote. I've lost a lot of family members, but usually it was a prolonged thing and you're ready for it. . . . It so touched me that I was just like, it's one thing if you forgive them five years from now, but it was hours. These parents, it's like they're the salt of the earth. If only so many other people could be like that, and have that capacity for forgiveness, the world would be such a better place. It was amazing."

Rybak hesitated at first to send her work to the Snyders. She waited six months before mailing her metaphorical message in a bottle. Only after being contacted for this book did she learn that the Snyders had received it and recognized what she did as a special act.

"I wasn't even expecting anything," she said, recounting how she got goose bumps when she learned the Snyders' reaction. "For me, my piece is complete. I've come full circle in completing this artwork . . . When push comes to shove, if it's meant to reach them, it will reach them. If not, I'll never know."

10/11/03
. . . I never got a chance to see Dan play and never really knew who he was until a few months ago.
— Ashley Marie Poitras, 14 years old,
Weston, Fla.

❋

We lost our 21-year-old daughter in a car accident this spring. We understand the devastating grief and sorrow you are feeling. We pray God will help you as you struggle to live each day.
—Tony and Jane Mulder and family

❋

Feb. 6, 2005
. . . You have caused me to examine my own
behaviour and reactions and have taught me so
much. I know I'm not alone in this . . .
  — Anne-Marie Borthwick, Toronto

❋

. . . After my first half season with Owen Sound, I
decided to go and explore pro hockey in the U.S.
instead of playing my overage year. Halfway
through that season, I began to get the odd phone
call from Dan hinting at me to come back to the
team. He slowly planted the seed in my head, and
finally at the end of one of the calls I gave in and
decided to go back to Owen Sound. Plus, I didn't
want him to miss any of the game vs. Plymouth
because he was calling in between periods from the
coach's office. It meant a lot to me that he kept
calling and convinced me to come back to give me
the chance to play with my leader, my captain and
my friend again.

Since playing together in junior we got the
chance to meet up a couple of times. There were
two times that I remember the most because they
were big points in both of our lives. One was when
he had signed with Atlanta and we all got together
to celebrate, and the second was at my stag and
doe where he came to show his support.

We will remember Dan with the fondest of
memories and consider ourselves lucky to have

known him. You should be extremely proud of the person he was in everyone's eyes.

Sincerely,
— Mike and Laura Lankshear

✳

My son, Rob Brown, had the opportunity of playing with Dan in Chicago, and spoke of him so often and relayed several funny stories about he and Dan. I felt like I knew him, too.

I lost a daughter a few years ago as a result of a car accident, and I know what you are going through. I truly feel sorry for both of you. The pain does diminish as time goes by, and you will be able to smile when you remember Dan and things that he did . . . .

I hope you gain some comfort from this.
Sincerely,
— Karen MacKenzie

✳

. . . I have the picture of your radiant face etched in my memory. You were beaming as you told me of Dan's call home — he had received the good news from his coach. Your son had achieved the goal for which he had worked. He was thrilled and you were proud . . . .

May you feel God's sustaining love and healing.
— Virginia Frau

CHAPTER 13

SUMMER INTO FALL

Lynn Vaughn is a former anchor for CNN's Headline News who has a cheery outlook. In the summer of 2004, she was filling in as a public relations officer in the Fulton County District Attorney's office for the regular spokesman, who was on leave. Despite her disposition, she appeared flustered and surprised by the interest the Heatley case received in Canada and the many inquiries she received from north of the border. Limited by what she could say when queried by reporters as to when Dany Heatley might be indicted, she would stick to saying things like, "The grand jury meets on Tuesdays and Fridays." When one Canadian outlet took that to mean Heatley would be indicted on one of those following Tuesdays or Fridays, she had trouble comprehending how she had been misunderstood.

On the morning of July 16, Vaughn delivered the word to

the news media that it had long awaited. Fulton County District Attorney Paul Howard would hold a news conference that day at 2 p.m. At that time, Howard announced that the grand jury had returned a six-count indictment against Heatley, including a charge of homicide by vehicle in the first-degree, a felony which was supported by a charge of reckless driving, and a charge of homicide by vehicle in the second-degree, which was supported by the count of driving too fast for conditions. Howard said that, if convicted on the felony charge, Heatley would face three to fifteen years in jail. The stakes were high.

"I would like to say that in our community, all citizens must be held accountable when they ignore traffic laws which are designed to protect and safeguard all of us," Howard said. "There's no one here who probably hasn't driven over the speed limit at one time or the other. But this case is different, in that it involves extreme speed when taken into context of this curving, well-travelled road in a residential area. This is clearly a tragic example, and I believe, for our whole community, and especially our young people, of how horrible the consequences can be for an innocent victim like Daniel Snyder when a driver chooses to ignore common safety rules."

In using the code words "extreme speed," Howard was laying out the crux of his case for seeking a first-degree charge. The speed limit on Lenox Road is 35 miles per hour. The initial police report said Heatley was travelling at 82 miles per hour. The District Attorney's commitment to a high speed would ultimately play an instrumental role in how the case would play out.

"What's important in this case is that there does not have to be a specific speed," he offered. "The specific speed involves driving past the posted speed limit. And whatever the speed was, it was exceeded."

Reporters queried Howard as to his motivation in seeking the indictment. Was he seeking to exonerate himself for what many saw as the botched prosecution of the case of NFL all-pro linebacker Ray Lewis? Howard scoffed at the notion, refusing to acknowledge any correlation between the two. Why was he prosecuting Heatley when the victim's family did not want to see Heatley go to jail?

The answer to that question brought one of the more puzzling responses of the session. In referring to his office's conversations with Dan Snyder's mother — to whom he referred as "Linda" — Howard said, "Well, we have had some conversations with the Snyder family, and that is not what the Snyder family has said to us. What Mrs. Snyder said is she realized we had our obligation as prosecutors and she expected that we would exercise and carry out that obligation. So that is not what we have received from the Snyder family — that they were opposed. What they made clear is that they simply did not want to take part in the trial."

Those comments baffled most in the room. The Snyders released a statement through the Thrashers the same day that read, "Our feelings have never changed, and we continue to support Dany and the entire Heatley family. Despite our personal feelings in this matter, we respect the responsibility of the district attorney's office and the legal process." If that seemed at all ambiguous, Graham Snyder was contacted at his home in Elmira to clarify after Howard's news conference.

"It's not our wishes," Graham Snyder said. "But we do respect the [district attorney's] office and their duties."

In Calgary, Heatley and his family stayed as far away from

N

reporters as they could. That left Heatley's agent, Stacey McAlpine, to act as the family's spokesman. "I think we're all trying to maintain a positive outlook on things," McAlpine said. "I think, too, that although the news is disappointing, we're still hopeful that a happy resolution will be found."

A law professor at Georgia State University, Mark Kadish, a former partner of Heatley's attorney Ed Garland, spoke to the *Atlanta Journal–Constitution* about the dilemma that Howard faced, which was tinged by racial politics and the memory of the Lewis trial. "If he doesn't prosecute him, people would say: 'The white celebrity got away because he's a celebrity.' Whereas, if he was a black man from the ghetto, he would be prosecuted."

Ryan Christie got married the day after Dany Heatley was indicted. Dan Snyder was supposed to have been Christie's best man. Snyder's family were invited guests at the ceremony. Christie, in his understated manner, made a toast that day to his friend.

"It was pretty tough," he said. "I was trying to make my speech for thanking everyone for coming and all that. It was pretty tough when I had to thank the Snyder family and wish Dan was there. . . . I just thanked the Snyders for coming and said something nice like, 'We all wish Dan could be here, but we know he's watching.'"

For a few summers, Snyder lived with Christie at his home in Beamsville, Ontario, near Niagara Falls, and the two would train together. During their junior careers, Snyder and Christie would have Sundays off about once a month and travel to Elmira for a Sugar Kings game and dinner with

Snyder's parents. "They treated us like gold, so we kept going back," Christie said. "We were always at one another's place. His buddies became my buddies and my buddies became his."

The same became true of Christie and Jake Snyder. When the accident happened, Christie was playing for the AHL's Toronto Roadrunners. He learned of the news early on the morning of September 30, 2003, and went to practice anyway. One of his assistant coaches, Geoff Ward, had worked with Jeff Snyder on the staff of the Kitchener Rangers, and knew of Christie and Snyder's relationship. He told Ryan to go home and Christie took the next two weeks off, a time he described as a "blur." Like so many of Snyder's friends, Christie was kept apprised of his friend's health by Jake Snyder.

"I know it was hard for him," Christie said. "It was hard for me to listen. It was hard not to break down. I'd have the top of the phone away from my head, trying to listen so he couldn't hear my reaction to anything. He was pretty strong. He helped me a lot."

With the Snyders in Atlanta and him in Toronto, Christie did not see the family until Dan's wake at the funeral home. Graham Snyder spotted him at the back of the long line and motioned him to come forward but Christie waited. When he finally got to the front, Graham greeted the speechless Christie with a hug. Then Jake Snyder spoke to him. "Jake said, 'He thought of you as a brother, too,'" Christie said. "He started crying again. LuAnn, they all kept saying I was part of the family and that meant a lot. . . . His family's been amazing for everybody. They shouldn't be the ones who are comforting other people and they are. Normally, you try to help people through their tough time. They tried to do it the other way. It just makes you shake your head. It's just the way they are."

For a time, when Christie was with Kalamazoo and Snyder was with Orlando, the friends were opponents in the IHL. "We both played pretty hard," Christie said. "It hurt a lot more when we fought against each other — when he whacked me in the back of the legs or in the arm. But at the end of the game, we'd go out for dinner. That's when you know you've got a pretty good friend. I think that maybe he took it easy on me, I don't know."

Like any of Snyder's friends, Christie has memorable stories. Christie remembers Snyder wanting to go to a Metallica concert — but only if they dressed up in cut-off jean jackets and black leather pants. Christie skipped the pants. He also recalled Snyder for imitating a scene out of the Chris Farley film, *Tommy Boy*. Snyder would find an especially effeminate looking woman's jacket, then put it on for laughs just at the right moment.

"Every once in a while, he'd have a bar cleared out, or there would be a circle around Dan so he could put on his show," Christie said. "He was priceless." Christie said he tries not to dwell on his friend's death too much. But at times, a thought will pass through his head and he will want to call Snyder to tell him. "I'd love to give him a call, but I can't do that. It happens quite a bit. That's the hardest part."

The reason prosecutors spoke to LuAnn Snyder prior to Heatley's indictment was that Graham and Jake were not in Elmira at the time. They had gone on a two-week tour of Major League Baseball cities, attending 10 games in 12 days along the east coast. The original idea was that Dan was to have gone with them on the trip. In his absence, they decided to follow through anyway. "It was definitely a good time to get away for myself and my dad," Jake said. "We had done a lot in the media. It was nice to spend two weeks as father and son and get away to something like that we enjoy, seeing a lot of states and cities we've never been to. We went to Maine and ate lobster. I had three lobsters." Graham and Jake went to Yankee Stadium and Fenway Park, where Jarrod Skalde had arranged, through Andy Brickley, the former NHL player turned Boston Bruins broadcaster, for them to sit in a box. Curt Schilling pitched for Boston the same season the perennial hard-luck loser Red Sox won their first World Series since 1918. Jake owns a Red Sox cap and when asked about it, he gave an answer with a double meaning: "I pull for the underdog" — an allusion to his brother. The trip was successful enough that Jake and Graham decided they'd try to make it an annual affair.

A few days after Heatley's indictment, Jake hit the road again. The second trip also involved sports and his brother. Thrashers assistant equipment manager Joey Guilmet is a native of San Diego, and prior to the accident, Guilmet had suggested that Snyder and some others make a guys-only trip to opening day at the thoroughbred racetrack in Del Mar. The track sports a classy scene, and the Pacific Ocean provides a gorgeous backdrop.

With Snyder's passing, his friends decided to travel to California anyway, much as his father and brother had done with the baseball trip. Dany Heatley flew in, as did Skalde, who brought his wife. When Dan died, Guilmet took his death as hard as anyone. He and Dan shared an interest in music. No matter the band or style of music — anything from the Dave Matthews Band to the hard rock of Atlanta band Sevendust

— Guilmet could always count on Snyder to come with him to a club, whether it was in Atlanta or on the road. It was Guilmet who had arranged for Snyder's guitar lessons in Atlanta, from a musician friend of his. When Guilmet and his wife, Kim, bought their first house in Atlanta, Snyder was their first visitor.

"When we bought our house we were so proud," Guilmet said. "The day we closed, we went over there at five o'clock, and he came by with Lisa, his girlfriend. We had just closed up an hour or two before, and it meant so much to me that he went out of his way to come by. And he was like, 'Geez, Joey, this is so awesome.' He was so proud for us."

Amidst the stylish crowd at Del Mar, Snyder's friends honoured him by emulating his quirky style. They all wore hockey jerseys in loud combinations with shorts, while nearby women wore cocktail dresses. "He did that from when he was four or five years old 'til the day he died," Jake said. "That was the way he was. He'd like to get a laugh out of people. I don't always think it was for attention. He liked to make other people laugh. It was something he'd always done. He'd be at a party — and it didn't even have to be a costume party — and he'd show up in something stupid, just the dumber the better."

Jake wore one of Dan's old Quebec Nordiques jerseys with the number 17 — his brother's number through minor hockey — and "Dan" printed on the back. Skalde wore another of Dan's Nordiques jerseys, which was about 15 years old and skin-tight on its newest wearer. One of Guilmet's brothers wore a Capitals sweater. Someone else wore an old Winnipeg Jets jersey and was cheered by a member of the crowd: "Go Jets!" They partied in Dan's memory.

"We stuck out like sore thumbs," Guilmet recalled. "That

will be our trip every year. It was a good time. I tried to explain to these guys what it's like." Heatley was able to relax, too, and get his mind off of his new legal troubles. A few days later, Guilmet took him to a San Diego Padres game, and got Heatley into the clubhouse through some friends of his. Heatley took batting practice and knocked some balls out of the park.

The rest of the summer was quiet. After the NHL season ended, Heatley, eager to play more hockey and continue to rebuild his prodigious skills, had been dominant at the World Championships in the Czech Republic, leading Canada to the title and earning the tournament's most valuable player award. That performance might have helped him earn a spot on Canada's August entry in the World Cup — another prestigious honour in his young career.

Canada did not have to leave home for a single game in the tournament and several of the games were played in Toronto. For those games, Heatley's family stayed with Graham and LuAnn one night, and the group attended several games together. At a Team Canada event Graham and LuAnn met Wayne Gretzky. LuAnn recalled the subject of Dan coming in a brief conversation with Gretzky, who shook his head and said, "I'm sorry." After Canada defeated the Finns for the tournament title, Jake met Dan's idol, Joe Sakic.

On the ice, Heatley played on Canada's most productive line of the tournament, with Ryan Smyth and Vincent Lecavalier, who ended up as the tournament's most valuable player, leading Canada to victory. Heatley contributed, but also visibly struggled at times, with only two assists in six games while his linemates entered the championship game as the first- and third-highest scorers on the team.

"I'm sure he doesn't have the goals he'd like to have and contribute in that way, but he does other things that spark the line or the hockey club," Smyth said. "With all of the stuff he's going through, he could shut her down and pack it in, but he's prevailed through a lot of adversity in life and throughout the game, and he competes hard every night." In celebrating the final 2–1 victory over Finland, Heatley basked in one of the top accomplishments of his career. It was another moment that allowed him a respite from the previous month's events.

Two days after the World Cup, the NHL began the lockout that would wipe out the entire 2004–05 season — the first North American professional sports league to cancel a season over a labour dispute. Like virtually all NHL players, Heatley remained in limbo. About a month after the lockout began, he signed with SC Bern of the Swiss League, where he would play alongside the Buffalo Sabres' Daniel Briere, whom he befriended six months earlier playing for Team Canada in the World Championships. The day word leaked to the media that he had signed with Bern, the Atlanta Hawks were playing a pre-season game in Macon, Georgia, against the Orlando Magic. Coincidentally, Fulton County District Attorney Paul Howard was in attendance to watch his nephew Dwight Howard, the first overall pick in that summer's NBA draft. From his seat in the Macon Coliseum, Howard saw nothing to prevent Heatley from playing in Europe, just as he had not stood in Heatley's way during the previous NHL season or the

World Championships. "The judge gave him an opportunity to make bond," Howard said. "It would be comparable to any other defendant getting another job. When the trial starts — if there is a trial — he will have to stand for trial."

Those words would prove providential. Heatley would have a lone pretrial hearing — on November 29 — before the case would either have to be settled or go to trial in February. He was present at the hearing at a time when he was not playing hockey, having suffered a serious injury earlier in the month playing for Bern. After undergoing surgery in Switzerland, he returned home for several weeks, occasionally consulting an eye specialist in Vancouver. It was Briere, ironically, who'd hit Heatley in the eye with a shot as Heatley fell to the ice in front of the opposing goal. The November hearing was not auspicious for Heatley. Prosecutor Brett Pinion had introduced into evidence the fact that Heatley had not paid a speeding ticket he received for driving 88 miles per hour on I-24 in Kentucky, where the speed limit was 65. The ticket, which Heatley received before his September 29, 2003, accident, led to the suspension of his licence.

One thing that went in Heatley's favour was the judge's decision to rule inadmissible a 2002 fender-bender, in which Heatley was cited for following too closely behind another driver. The previous month, the judge had ruled that any evidence relating to Heatley's blood-alcohol level would also be inadmissible, as the quantity he consumed was insignificant. The judge waited to decide on a more damaging allegation: that a woman had accused Heatley of driving so aggressively in the weeks before the crash that she called 911. However, no police report was filed in the alleged incident, and Heatley was not charged. Perhaps Judge Rowland Barnes was waiting to rule as an incentive for Heatley's lawyers to make a deal with the prosecutor.

With just a little more than two months before the trial was set to begin, the prosecution was hardly yielding, and Dany Heatley did not have much wiggle room.

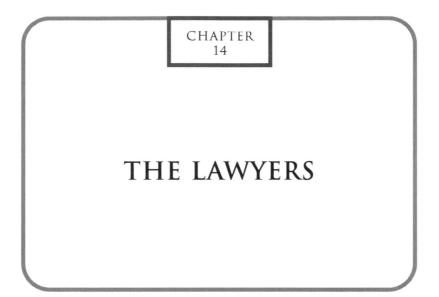

THE LAWYERS

The weather for Super Bowl xxxiv in Atlanta was uncommonly harsh. Ice storms and temperatures around freezing are not what the NFL expects when it awards its jewel to a southern city. It also does not envision a public relations disaster wherein one of its marquee stars is involved in a murder in the hours following its season-crowning event.

In the days before the Super Bowl, Baltimore Ravens All-Pro linebacker Ray Lewis rented a 40-foot Lincoln Navigator limousine and partied during the nearly 700-mile trip south. In Atlanta, he met up with with longtime associates Joseph Sweeting and Reginald Oakley. The destination was the city's Buckhead district, which, with cavernous mansions built on spacious tree-filled lots on private winding streets, has become home to African-American recording artists, professional athletes and entertainers, helping to earn Atlanta a reputation as a welcoming place for African-Americans around the country. The city, the home of Dr. Martin Luther King Jr., earned that status during the civil rights movement, when it remained relatively calm amid a cauldron of explosive social forces. Over the years, as the metropolitan area grew from a sleepy southern city to one of the nation's most populous areas, Atlanta became known for its tolerance and progressive attitude, and in the process, it became attractive to members of the gay community, as well as African-Americans. As a result, the city's nightlife — with restaurants like Justin's, partly owned by rapper/record producer Sean "P. Diddy" Combs, and clubs such as the now-closed Cobalt lounge — has spots that cater to the well-heeled African-American crowd.

In the early morning hours of January 31, 2000, Lewis, Sweeting and Oakley gravitated towards this scene, and Cobalt. The club designated Sunday nights "urban" nights, hoping to attract a specific crowd. Club owner Charles Cook described the Sunday night crowd of predominantly African-Americans to the *Atlanta Journal–Constitution*: "They drink hundreds of bottles of cognac at $10 a glass. I'm constantly running out of $400 and $500 bottles of champagne, because that's what they prefer. My club's so popular that we had to shut the door down for an hour Sunday night because so many people wanted to get in. It's a wonderful thing for the affluent African-American community."

Heightening the atmosphere at the club on the night of January 31, 2000, was the Super Bowl, which serves as a sort of annual roving circus and a magnet for celebrities of all kinds. Earlier in the week, Falcons running back Jamal Anderson had hosted an event at the club which was attended by Wayne

Gretzky, Michael Jordan, John Elway and Leonardo DiCaprio; Peyton Manning was reportedly turned away at the door.

That night was Lewis's first visit to Cobalt. Also partying at the club that night (after the St. Louis Rams held off the Tennessee Titans in a thrilling finish at the Georgia Dome) and willing to pay the $100 per person cover charge were Jacinth Demarus "Shorty" Baker, 21, and Richard Dameco Lollar, 24. The men had grown up together in Akron, Ohio, and had moved to Atlanta in the preceding years. Baker earned his nickname from standing 5-foot-1. Lollar was engaged to be married — his fiancée was pregnant at the time and he worked 12-hour shifts at a barbershop.

Over the course of the evening, Baker and Lollar's paths crossed with those of Lewis and his friends, and an argument broke out. Just before 4 a.m. on the morning of the 31st, Lewis left the club with an entourage of about 10 male and female acquaintances. Lewis's lawyer — Ed Garland — would later accuse Baker, Lollar and a third man of harassing the Lewis crowd outside the club. As he was getting into the limousine, Sweeting was hit in the head with a champagne bottle. Two blocks away from the club, a melee erupted. Witnesses would alternately describe six or 10 people flailing about. Knives were pulled. Baker suffered a four-inch gash in his abdomen and died at the hospital. Lollar died at the scene. In the chaos, Lewis and his cohorts fled into the limousine. Bullets struck the vehicle, with one hitting the right front tire.

Less than two weeks after the murders, a Fulton County grand jury indicted Lewis, Oakley and Sweeting each on two counts of murder, felony murder and aggravated assault with a deadly weapon. District Attorney Paul Howard said he would consider the death penalty for all three.

A graduate of Morehouse College, Atlanta's prestigious, historically black college, and Emory University law school, Howard worked eight years as a prosecutor in the Fulton County office before becoming a defence lawyer. In 1996, he won election as the county's district attorney. So by the time the 48-year-old Howard chose to prosecute Lewis himself when the legal action began in May 2000, he had not tried a case in four years.

But even before the trial began, the prosecution took some missteps. Under the intense glare of the national media in the high-profile case, Howard sought the indictment before the investigation was complete — a move that would greatly hamper his case. Less than one week after Lewis was indicted, his legal team, led by Garland and Don Samuel — the same lawyers Dany Heatley would employ three years later — filed what is known as a speedy trial motion, which dictated that the case would begin by June, less than three and a half months away. The case was so rushed by the prosecution that the district attorney's office was still interviewing witnesses during the trial. By comparison, Howard would wait more than nine months after Dan Snyder died — until his investigation was complete — before indicting Heatley on first- and second-degree vehicular homicide charges.

Once the Lewis trial began in mid-May, the media circus was in full bloom. Court TV broadcast the trial, with former NFL players Lynn Swann and Tim Green on the scene. ESPN also was present. Local channels covered the trial heavily and, as it is based in Atlanta, CNN was ready to feature any breaking news. From the start, the prosecution faced a difficult task. For one, a witness had seen someone hit Sweeting in the head with a champagne bottle. The testimony cast Lollar and Baker as possible aggressors, weakening Howard's case. And further, witnesses were not exactly lining up to accuse a millionaire pro football player, and codefendants with long criminal histories.

Early in the trial, things started going against Howard. The prosecution's star witness was the limousine driver, Duane Fassett. On the stand, Fassett was the antithesis of the enthusiastic witness, and his testimony did little to bolster the prosecution's case. In statements to police, Fassett had said he saw Lewis punch one of the victims in the midsection and that he had heard Oakley say, "I stabbed mine," and Sweeting say, "I stabbed mine, too." When Fassett failed to reinforce that testimony on the stand, Howard failed to challenge him on it — which some critics saw as a glaring error.

A little over a week after Fassett testified, Lewis had his plea deal. Garland and Samuel had gotten him off without jail time. Lewis had the charges reduced to the misdemeanor of obstruction of justice, was sentenced to 12 months probation, and forced to pay one-third the costs incurred by the prosecution, about $40,000. That was nothing compared to the $1 million his legal defence cost him, but it kept him free. Addressing reporters' questions about the arrangement, Howard confessed to being disappointed and surprised by the testimony of some witnesses.

The best Ray Lewis could do on the stand, once he'd taken his plea and testified against his former friends, was to say that he saw Oakley hitting Baker, but that he did not see a knife in Oakley's hands. Lewis testified that Sweeting told him he hit the victims, and that he'd later seen a knife in Sweeting's hands, but, again, did not testify to seeing him stab Lollar. In his three hours of testimony, Lewis said he never saw Sweeting nor Oakley stab the victims. In fact, in the end, both men were acquitted, shocking the community. Two murders and no one was held accountable — except for Lewis, with his misdemeanor and suspended sentence. Sweeting and Oakley celebrated by visiting Atlanta's Gold Club, a notorious strip club that closed years later after a federal racketeering trial. In that trial, prosecutors aired the dirty laundry of Madonna, the King of Sweden and actor Stephen Baldwin. Ex-New York Knick Patrick Ewing and Braves centrefielder Andruw Jones also testified as to their sordid activities there. One of the codefendants in that trial was represented by Don Samuel.

Rutherford Seydel learned of Dany Heatley's accident around 5 a.m. on the morning of September 30, 2003. In the previous weeks, Seydel, a prominent Atlanta lawyer, had helped to form a group to purchase the Hawks, Philips Arena and the Thrashers from Time Warner. Along with some local businessmen, and others from Boston and Washington, Seydel, a longtime Hawks season-ticket holder, put together a deal to snatch away the properties from Texas businessman David McDavid, who had previously held the exclusive negotiating rights to purchase them. McDavid, who was financing the deal, worth hundreds of millions of dollars, became vulnerable as the negotiations took on a glacial pace, allowing his exclusivity clause to lapse. Seydel's group paid cash — $244 million — and the final agreement was done in weeks.

Less than one week after the sale, Seydel found himself at

Grady Hospital trying to locate Heatley and Snyder, who were in rooms under assumed names. Using his connections to find them, his first instinct was to see if he could help put the players in touch with any of Atlanta's best doctors or medical facilities such as the Shepherd Center, which specializes in spinal injuries.

"It became clear that the doctors were doing a great job," Seydel said. "The families were not there yet but they were coming from Canada."

Reassured that Snyder and Heatley were receiving the medical assistance they needed, Seydel turned next to his area of expertise to help the players: his legal contacts. Whenever he visited Heatley, he said Heatley's concern was for Snyder, but Seydel was also aware of the legal burden Heatley would soon face. "My strong advice was that he be thinking about this," Seydel said. "I said, 'I know you don't want to think about that right now, but . . .'" So Seydel took it upon himself to scroll through his cell phone directory and call Ed Garland, a friend of his parents from the days when they attended high school together. Seydel and Garland also are involved in several Atlanta charitable organizations together.

"One of the highlights of the Christmas season is Eddy's huge Christmas party," Seydel said. "My parents have known him for 40 or 50 years." Seydel did not want to meddle with the affairs of two Time Warner employees, so he said he called Garland for advice. "I said, 'I just want to tell you the facts and ask you what you think,'" Seydel said. "Then I called one of the Time Warner executives. . . . If I ever got in trouble, [Garland]'s the first person I'd call — whether I'd need his great services or not."

It was not long before Garland's firm of Garland, Samuel and Loeb was representing Heatley. On the most important cases, Ed Garland and Don Samuel work together. In the Heatley case, Garland led the defence, but Samuel was involved throughout. Among the chief obstacles Heatley's legal team would face was the fact that Heatley was a Canadian citizen. Jail time or a felony plea might lead to Heatley's being deported or ruled inadmissible by the U.S. Immigration and Naturalization Service, all but ending his NHL career. Samuel said the legal team realized that legal hurdle "immediately — as soon as we realized he was a Canadian citizen — about twenty minutes into the case."

Nonetheless, nearly nine months passed after the accident with virtually no activity — no indictment came. The lack of action left many in the media and the public at large to wonder what was going on, was the district attorney simply waiting for an opportune time, when no one was looking, to dismiss the charges? Perhaps the Lewis case was in the back of his mind, and the speedy trial motion filed by Garland and Samuel which proved so damaging to his case. But — whatever his motivation — Fulton County District Attorney Paul Howard took his time with the investigation of Dany Heatley. The anticipation of some kind of resolution to Heatley's legal status — either an indictment or a dismissal of the charges — was expected throughout the season. On December 26, 2003, the day Heatley first spoke publicly about the ordeal, Ed Garland told reporters he expected the prosecution to complete its investigation in "30 to 45 days." But Heatley returned to play a month later and the season ended. Heatley went on to play for Team Canada in the World Championships and still there was no indictment. Nearly nine months after the accident the indictment finally came.

Don Samuel said Heatley's legal team did not receive the Ferrari to begin its own investigation for eight to ten months, around the same time that Heatley was indicted on July 16. The most significant event to come out of the grand jury proceedings was that the district attorney had won an indictment on first-degree vehicular homicide and reckless driving, both of which were felonies. After the terrorist attacks of September 11, 2001, on the United States, the INS began looking more closely at persons convicted of certain crimes. Heatley was in a bit of a gray area — but he could not afford convictions or pleas to the most serious charges.

"It's not that the laws are new, but post 9/11 the degree to which they are enforced has increased dramatically," Samuel said. "It used to be, for most cases, you'd get bond and you wouldn't think about it for years, and the INS eventually would say, 'We don't care.' That kind of laissez-faire attitude came to an end. A minor drug offense would become not so minor."

One key witness on Heatley's side — a witness whose presence might have been enough to force the prosecution to settle the case favourably for Heatley — said he thought the district attorney had overreached with the charge of first-degree vehicular homicide. So often throughout Heatley's legal case, the public in Atlanta and throughout Canada believed he was receiving preferential treatment. But it's possible the reverse was the case.

"Probably, I think that's probably true," Samuel said. "When you have a motor vehicle death with no alcohol, generally it's not going to be first degree. Generally. By no means is that always the case. They tend to be drag races. [The reckless element], that's exactly what makes it [first degree]. But speeding can make it reckless. You tend to plead down to a misdemeanor. A single [car] wreck, I'd have to say it's very unusual to begin at first-degree. It's not unethical, it's just a general strategy. The D.A.'s not looking to make more trouble for themselves if the victim's [family] is not jumping up and down."

Is it unethical to go for a first-degree indictment despite evidence to the contrary? Samuel said he did not fault the district attorney for searching out other opinions. Nonetheless, the repercussions of the Ray Lewis case appear to cast a lingering shadow.

"No," Samuel said. "It would not be unusual for the D.A. to take a second expert's opinion at the highest possible charge with an eye towards settling. It's almost like a negotiating tactic. I'll go for the most I think I can support . . . that's a pretty typical litigation strategy. It can be abused if there's no evidence for the sole reason for negotiating down." Then he offered, unsolicited, "Ray Lewis . . ." and paused, "was unethical. What was unethical was that there was every reason to arrest him on suspicions and misrepresentations made to the police, but it became abundantly clear there was no case against him, and [Howard] wouldn't back down and went forward not trying to support the charge. That, I think, spills over into unethical behavior. But all's well that ends well."

In 1988, Tom Langley retired from the police force in Cobb County, the conservative suburb to Atlanta's northwest. As a police officer, he'd reconstructed more than 350 fatal accidents. After going to work as an expert who testifies mostly for the prosecution and at times in product-liability cases, he has reconstructed more than 1,000 fatal accidents and helped to train 24 agencies in Georgia, including the Atlanta Police Department and Georgia State Patrol. He has a sharp tongue and uses colourful language about those with whom he disagrees, saying of the Ray Lewis case: "Paul had looked like a fool." He said he'd warned the Atlanta police, "You guys have taken enough hits. You don't need to add this to your hall of shame." He speaks with confidence about his trade, as if he were physicist, though he only had two quarters of college education — in English. He is a law-and-order man and speaks with pride of putting away violators. Citing his background as a police officer, rarely would he work for the defence, especially someone like Ed Garland, a quintessential defence attorney.

In examining the thousands of documents of evidence in the prosecution's case against Heatley, Langley's name does not stand out. His work consists of a few photocopied pages of lined paper with calculations on them. On the first one is written "Heatley Speeds." Then the crucial sentence "If" — the word is underlined three times — "there were 100% braking across the mark?" Then a formula and "56.14 mph." The only place Langley's name appears is on a map he made for the police.

Samuel, of Heatley's legal team, said Langley's presence was "extraordinarily important" in settling the case. "His name was given to us in the original package of discovery," Samuel said. "It was not as clear as it should've been what he told the D.A.'s office by the original discovery we got. In the process of going through that, we finally got it. He came to the office and spent some time with us. That became important to the D.A. — that there was a lack of unanimity as to what the speed was. . . . That there were experts — and not the ones we hired — who were willing to say the speed was 60 or less."

Three days after Dany Heatley's crash, Langley mapped the scene. He said he did it at the request of the Atlanta Police Department — a statement that the Fulton County District Attorney's office would later deny. (They said they asked Langley to use his "equipment," a $14,000 machine called a "total station" which uses a laser to map contours of skid marks, gradients in the road and other physical characteristics of an accident scene. In an interview, Paul Howard said Langley was brought to the scene "out of abundance of caution" by a "police department in transition," as the Atlanta Police Department did not possess a "total station." In fact, Savannah, Georgia, attorney Mark Tate donated a "total station" to the Atlanta Police Department in April 2003, almost six months before Heatley's accident. Tate said he acted at the suggestion of Tom Langley.)

After mapping the scene on Friday, October 3, and computing Heatley's speed, Langley's conclusions were startling — but they never became public because the District Attorney chose not to follow up and ask Langley to write a report to go with them. Unlike Sergeant Hensal, who placed Heatley's speed at 82 miles per hour, Langley estimated Heatley's speed at between 56 and 58 miles per hour when Heatley lost control of the car. But Langley questioned Hensal's expertise — and for good reason. One of Heatley's attorneys, Manny Arora, said his office found documentation during its investigation that Hensal had not completed classes required to become an accident investigator at the time of the accident. After doing his calculations, Langley said he told the District Attorney's office, in the form of assistant D.A. Brett Pinion, that they did not have grounds for a first-degree charge against Dany Heatley.

Many points of the case remained in dispute among the prosecution, the defence and Langley — even after the resolution of the case. One example is that Pinion said Langley did deem Heatley's driving to be "reckless," which is a felony that supported the first-degree felony charge of vehicular homicide. Pinion said the prosecutors went so far as to hold a meeting with their appellate division to debate whether Langley could be asked at trial whether he believed Heatley's speed was reckless, which is normally a question that would have to be decided by the jury. "We wanted to be able to ask him, even though the speed is 55 [as calculated by Langley] and not 82, would you still consider it as reckless?" Paul Howard said. "He told us yes. So that is why when Brett and those talked to him we had our appellate section in and we met just to discuss can we get that testimony in?" The District Attorney said it found its own experts who challenged the accuracy of Langley's work, including a "consultant" — Western New England College professor emeritus of forensic physics John Kwasnoski, who was brought in in addition to the District Attorney's own expert. Conversely, Heatley's lawyers said their experts found more problems in the work done by the prosecution's experts, the primary example of which was a report commissioned by Knott Laboratories in Denver that placed Heatley's speed at between 86 and 95 miles per hour.

"I knew they had one guy out of Denver [Stephen Fenton]," Langley said. "The A.D.A. handling it, Brett, he told me he had it up to almost 90. I said, 'There's no way. Unless they hit Stone Mountain [the likeness of Confederate leaders carved into the side of the rock face located 15 miles from the Lenox Road site] at the end of that skid. You put [Fenton] up there on the stand and I'll tear his ass apart. He's making up science as he goes."

Langley said both the Knott Laboratories report, as well as the one filed by Sergeant Hensal, were flawed. And Langley said the diagram Knott used — with Hensal's name on it — was actually his work. He put Hensal's name on it to cover for the officer when he submitted the report. The District Attorney's office's explanation for the appearance of Langley's name on one of the maps of the scene that was accepted into evidence — a map that was identical to the one with Hensal's name on it that Knott Laboratories used in its report — was that in using Langley's equipment, the Atlanta Police officer never removed a template that had Langley's name on it. Langley said the machine does not have a template and that Hensal would not even know how to operate the software. Langley said that when Mark Tate donated the total station to the Atlanta Police Department, he donated two days of training, but to operate the machine properly, 40 hours are necessary.

"Hensal's not an expert," Langley said. "He's a police officer. He made the fatal mistake of going out there that night and making estimations based on the first blush. You see something torn up like that and go and tell the AP and the UPI and everybody he's going 80 to 85, and he hadn't done the first scientific research. [Police traffic investigator] Dave Kelley asked me to come down there and map it for him, and I got it in scale. After I did it, I got looking at it and did the speeds to satisfy my own curiosity. I called them and [Assistant D.A. Shondeana Crews] the next week, and told them I don't know where you're coming up with 80 or 85. . . .

"I did this as a favour for Atlanta P.D. I told them, 'Guys, with all the black eyes and bruises you've been getting, you don't need any more. Here's the speed. I do this every day for a living. The numbers are way too high.' It was flawed from the get-go. Pinion knew that, and another A.D.A., Paul Howard, wasn't interested in retaining my services since he already had an expert. I didn't get in his head. I didn't ask. The point of it is, 'I'll let you make a copy of my speed calculations and you show them to whoever you want. Until you pay me for my time, you can't use it any other way.' They weren't interested."

The crux of Langley's argument as to why Hensal and Knott are incorrect is that they used the wrong formula to compute Heatley's speed. They used a formula known as "critical speed," while Langley uses one called "kinetic energy." To use the critical speed formula, several criteria must be met. One of them is that the driver did not brake. Langley contends that Heatley braked. The District Attorney, not surprisingly, disagreed with that contention. "I don't recall him disputing it," Paul Howard said. "The reason I remember this is while we were negotiating with them, they brought that up, something about the brakes. This what I said to them: 'Whoa, if that's what you're contending, let's not even talk about any plea. Because I'm not taking a plea based on something that is just not true.' As I recall, they had a report or something or they were going to call an expert or something and they immediately said, 'We're not going to do that. Forget about it.'" Howard said Ed Garland made a special trip to his office one day and waited until 7:30 p.m. to inform him the defence would not dispute evidence about braking. "He came down and said, 'Ignore that, Paul. Don't pay any attention to that. Just assume you never even got that information.'" Heatley's attorney Manny Arora disputes this: "We didn't accept their version of the facts at all. We agreed we were speeding. Our 55 or 56 was clearly speeding . . . We knew we were going to hammer them on the speed [at trial]."

On December 16, 2003, the district attorney sent the anti-lock brake system (ABS) from the Ferrari to Robert Bosch Corporation in Michigan for testing. Specifically, inside the ABS is something called an electronic control unit, or ECU. Bosch's report is dated February 17, 2004. Under "Bosch analysis" it reads: "A 'fault code' refers to an information code that is set in the ECU when a condition is present that disables the ABS system and defaults the braking system to normal brake mode without ABS functionality. When an ABS fault code is set, other information supporting the fault code is also stored (i.e. vehicle speed, brake applied)." Then, under "Results of Bosch Analysis" the report reads: "Bosch's analysis of the ECU determined that there were no fault codes during and as a result of the accident." All that proved was that the brakes did not malfunction, but it could not settle questions of whether or not the brakes were applied. It also did not reveal Heatley's speed, as the prosecutors had hoped.

Regardless, Langley criticized other aspects of the accident investigation. "They didn't look at the tail lights," he said, "they didn't do forensics of the injuries, they didn't check the brake pedal to see if it had marks from the bottom of his foot, which they could've done. They didn't have the ability to prove he's not braking." The district attorney pointed out that, unlike its own experts, Langley never examined the car.

But even someone who isn't an expert can find Langley's arguments persuasive. With the kinetic energy formula, a reconstructionist can estimate how much speed the car absorbed as it crashed. Increasingly, Langley said, cars are built to absorb crashes: they crumple, taking the impact so the passenger does not and survives. If Heatley had been driving at 85 or 90 miles per hour, Langley said, the remains of the Ferrari would have travelled much farther than the six or eight feet from the brick pillar where they stopped — thus his Stone Mountain comment. He said the remains of the car would have had to skid much farther to dissipate the remaining speed the car had at the time of impact.

Langley also contends that there might have been something faulty with the Ferrari. "It shouldn't have split," he said. "The faulty part is you're either looking at welds breaking or splitting in half, or there was not enough structural rigidity to absorb the impact. . . . In this case, the car wasn't strong enough to stay together. Why did it tear apart?"

Picking through the case file, Garland and his attorneys kept coming across Langley's name. They called him before Christmas 2003, and found an ace in the hole. The way the case was being handled infuriated Langley enough to work for Garland. He was never paid his fee of less than $3,000 by the district attorney's office for mapping the scene, and said he never received any compensation from Garland.

"I'm a retired police sergeant out of Cobb County. I retired 17 years ago, and I'm very pro-police," Langley said. "I don't do criminal defence. I turn my nose up at getting off people who are killing people. But I told Atlanta P.D. three days post-crash, and I told the D.A., and they still decided to go ahead and bury their head in the sand. When Garland called, I said, 'All bets are off.' I don't mind helping him. If I were in Cobb, I'd prosecute [Heatley] on second-degree all day. He's guilty as sin. I also told the D.A. and I told Garland, 'You know what? He didn't lose control because of the curve and speed in the curve. He was physically trying to avoid someone coming out of a private driveway [leading to a townhome that was vacant at the time]. His tire marks start in the wrong place and go in the wrong direction for exceeding the speed limit. He should've gone outside and not inside the double yellow line. . . .

"Ed was tickled to hear I had done my work and that I had the opinions I had, because he was trying to take care of Dany. [At first] I wouldn't work for him. I didn't have this kind of involvement, I don't care how much money he's got. It's a business decision I've made a lot. Ed's a nice fellow. It's obvious he's got tons of money. He's very successful. He could pay whatever bill I had. And as an expert, my job isn't to prove or disprove. My job is to explain what the truth is, and a judge or jury decides. I really don't care one way or another. . . . I said, 'Guilty all day of second degree. Not a doubt in the world.' He wasn't drunk, reckless. It wasn't a hit-and-run. He didn't do anything to precipitate that charge. And I was a hard-ass in Cobb."

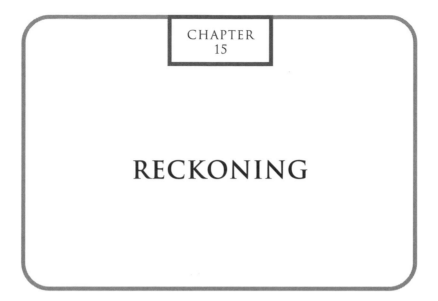

CHAPTER
15

RECKONING

Time passed with a nerve-wracking indolence for the Snyders in the final weeks before Dany Heatley's case was set to begin. From the outside, it appeared the case would be settled with a plea agreement that avoided a trial. Neither side wanted a trial: Heatley had too much to risk, as a conviction would have brought him an average sentence of five years in jail, and the prosecution would have had a tough sell with a jury that might wonder why Heatley should be convicted when the victim's family did not want him to be.

The way LuAnn Snyder described it, she was perpetually waiting for "the other shoe to drop." Two weeks before the trial was set to begin, Heatley's attorney Ed Garland told the media that he expected a deal could be struck in 48 hours. January 28 — one year to the date after Heatley had returned to the ice against the St. Louis Blues — loomed as the deadline for the parties to negotiate a plea. After that, Heatley's only option would be simply to plead guilty and hope the judge had mercy on him in meting out the sentence.

In yet another act of brinksmanship, two days later the parties extended their deadline to the following Friday. Sleep was difficult to come by for Graham Snyder and his family that first week of February. Jury selection for the trial was set to begin the following Monday. On January 31, the Snyders received the most positive sign to date from Fulton County District Attorney Paul Howard, albeit not from him directly. That night, Howard was attending an Atlanta Hawks game at Philips Arena against the Orlando Magic, the team his 19-year-old nephew Dwight plays for. In that setting, away from his office and his suit, and caught up in his enthusiasm for his nephew, he spoke plainly about the case.

"There are some things that are real important to the Snyder family," Howard said. "They made it very clear that they don't want to see [Heatley's] career interrupted or him go to jail. They made that quite clear. . . . It's very difficult because, let's say there is a trial and the judge had to sentence him, the judge is faced with sentencing someone who the victim's own family doesn't want to see his career interrupted. What we're trying to do is be realistic based on the circumstances and what the victim's family wants. It would be a totally different incident if it didn't involve friends. But they were friends, and we're trying to work around those options." That was the first time the Snyders had heard Howard say publicly that he would take their wishes into account.

In the same interview, Howard would foreshadow the way the case would ultimately be decided and the impact the

Snyders would have on it. However, at the time it was difficult to discern his meaning.

"We'll let the court worry about whatever sentence is recommended," he said. "When considering the sentence, it's difficult when you have the Snyder family in the posture they're in. Usually the victim's family demands a lot more strict treatment, and they're not standing there for the defendant." Most important to Howard was what he had stressed from the beginning: that he wanted Heatley "to be accountable."

"It's really important to the public, [Heatley] ought to be open about what happened," he said. "It's important to the community, the community of young people and children. Someone in his position, if he made a mistake, he should say it so others can profit from it."

The next day, while sitting at his office in Elmira, Graham Snyder received an e-mailed copy of Howard's remarks in the *Atlanta–Journal Constitution* from Dan Marr. Graham agreed with Howard that Heatley needed to be accountable. But in his mind, that had already happened.

"We expect Dany to take responsibility," he said. "We don't want to see him serve jail time or lose his career. And he's never given me the impression he doesn't want to take responsibility. Maybe that's because of the counsel he's getting and — I hate to use this word for it — the game he's involved in that he doesn't get to say those things. . . . He's never indicated to me he doesn't take responsibility for it." Graham had reason for optimism, yet he remained uneasy. The politics involved in the case — the comparison to the Ray Lewis case, the history between Garland and Howard — were too opaque for him to read. "It's sometimes hard to figure out the manoeuvrings and the reasons why things are happening, the political motivation," he said. "You try and analyze as best you can. You don't have a crystal ball. I can only go by what they tell me and that's not always clear."

Graham Snyder spent the day before he and his family were to leave for Atlanta crafting a victim impact statement. The entire family had a role in drafting it, but he was in charge of pulling it together and delivering it. Of all the public speaking engagements he had made since Dan's death, none would be so important, so personal, so emotional. Maybe that explained why he had writer's block.

The Snyders left for Atlanta early on the morning of February 3. In the afternoon, they met with Heatley's legal team, but by the end of the day, they were still unsure if the district attorney would drop the most serious of the charges against Heatley — felonies that could bring longer jail sentences and place Heatley's NHL career in the greatest jeopardy. So the following day when the Snyder family members, and Heatley and his supporters, entered Superior Court Judge Rowland Barnes' room number 8-H at 9:30 a.m., the atmosphere was tense.

Howard and his assistant Shondeana Crews were already seated when Ed Garland entered the courtroom, walked over to them and bent over to have a discussion. The threesome then approached Judge Barnes and they all headed for Barnes' chambers. When they returned, Heatley was led into the courtroom by his three lawyers, including Rutherford Seydel. A large Thrashers contingent in support of Heatley included Don Waddell, Bob Hartley, assistant coach Steve Weeks and various staff members, including Joey Guilmet. Eight television cameras stood watch over the proceedings from just behind the jury box.

Barnes had some housekeeping to do for other trials on his docket before the hearing began, but he made the news official that many expected when he said, "I understand this is going to be a plea." After a brief recess, Shondeana Crews began the process of Heatley's guilty plea at 10 minutes after 10, questioning the 24-year-old directly.

"It is the state's understanding that this is a non-negotiated plea," she said. She called Heatley forward. "Let me explain, Mr. Heatley, I know counsel has explained to you what a non-negotiated plea is all about. Let me go ahead and explain that directly to you on the record. Once I accept — if you enter a plea of guilty — once I accept your plea, if you don't like the sentence, you will not be able to withdraw your plea. Do you understand that, sir?"

Heatley responded that he understood.

Next, as if flexing its muscles, the state began to recite its evidence. Crews said that based on their expert's reconstruction, Heatley's speed was approximately 82 miles per hour at the time of the accident. She recounted how a second expert — Langley — put Heatley's speed at 55 miles per hour and a third estimated his speed at between 85 and 90 miles per hour.

When she concluded, Garland had his turn. He began by stating Heatley's desire to take responsibility, and acknowledged the tragic death of Snyder. He put Heatley in a sympathetic light and challenged the state's evidence. "Unfortunately, Your Honour, [Heatley] was thrown from the vehicle and suffered head injuries and was unconscious," Garland said. "He is not able to recall, and has no memory after turning right from Peachtree Road onto Lenox Road. He cannot state why the car went out of control." Then the attorney challenged one point of the state's evidence that became a key factor in resolving the case. Garland said the second expert cited by the state — Thomas Langley — did not post Heatley's speed at 55 miles per hour over the speed limit, but at 55 miles per hour.

"Well, I understand, Mr. Garland, that part of the basis for you all finally coming together was some discrepancy and debate, I suppose, amongst the experts as to what really did happen," Judge Barnes said.

In what appeared to be a prearranged move, Garland continued by motioning that the felonies — counts 1 and 2 — be dropped so that only the misdemeanors remained. Had the state objected — or the judge disallowed this step — Heatley's career would have been in serious danger. Garland then introduced an expert, Maria Odom, whom Heatley's defence team had hired to sort through the complex immigration issues he faced. When hired by Heatley's legal team, Odom was in private practice. But she had worked for the U.S. Immigration and Naturalization Service representing the government in deportation proceedings — precisely the kind of situation Heatley was seeking to avoid. "I have had a chance to review the indictment and have had a chance to review the statutes," Odom said. "Having reviewed counts three through six, it is my opinion that a guilty plea would not adversely affect Mr. Heatley's ability to either remain in the United States or be admitted in the future," she said. "I do not think that the statutory definition of those crimes fall into the categories of concern, which are a crime of violence or a crime involving moral turpitude, which is a term that we use in immigration law to describe certain crimes." She explained that while being deported from the United States was the main issue, Heatley could also face the problem of trying to return and not being allowed in. She also added, "I believe as an additional precaution, I believe that a sentence to confinement should also be avoided if at all possible."

Then Garland asked her opinion of what might happen if the felony counts were not removed. "Your Honour, I believe that counts one and two contain within the statute elements of reckless disregard for the safety of others and that would cause — I think that would increase the chance — that this will be considered a crime of violence. And it would render him both inadmissible and deportable from the United States." Under the circumstances, the judge tried at times to keep the mood light. He thanked Odom by saying, "You have taken a very difficult area of the law and reduced it to words that even I can understand."

When she stepped down, Garland presented evidence of Heatley's work in the community — how he visited hospitals and founded an organization affiliated with the Thrashers to help children with lymphoma and leukemia. Heatley attorney Manny Arora was brought forth to attest to the thousands of e-mails and letters of support the defence team had received on Heatley's behalf.

"Judge, just briefly they [the letters] simply describe his dedication to the community," Arora said. "Most athletes these days are pretty much spoiled. We have a 24-year-old young man that has gone above and beyond in giving back to the community. We've got boxes of letters here back at the office."

After Arora finished, Garland had one more task. "Your Honour, at this time the Snyders, the family of the deceased, have come here," he said. "And Mr. Graham Snyder, the father, and Jake Snyder, the brother of the deceased, wish to speak to the court."

Standing tall and erect and with his whitish hair and goatee, Graham Snyder could have been a character out of any great literary drama. His speech was testimony to his pride in his son but evoked the pain the ordeal had brought him; his words an attempt to forestall even greater sorrow by paradoxically defending the one held responsible for his son's death. He spoke haltingly, but his sense of purpose was evident.

"Your Honour and members of the court, I thank you for your patience and the time in allowing us to speak today. And we would like to speak about our son and brother Dan," he said. "Family and friends were always a priority for Dan. He was always there for you when you needed him most. Today a young man needs him. And since he can't be here, we will stand in his place. We don't know, and may never know, the exact sequence of events that took place on September 29, 2003. But we do know the outcome. Dan was taken away from us. And I'm reading now as a parent. As a parent, it's hard to describe how you feel when you have lost one of your children. It is hard to fully understand unless it has happened to you. Your wishes, your hopes, your dreams for your child's future, are gone in an instant forever. You think of the things that you're never going to have, no wedding, no grandchildren, no more holiday or family gatherings. There will always be an empty chair at the table.

"Our pride in Dan was immeasurable. As with most parents, his accomplishments were our accomplishments. They branched out to our immediate family, extended family and to our community. We will all miss him. He was a person who set goals for himself from the time that he was very small, and ultimately he achieved those goals.

"So how do we move on from here? The forgiveness in our hearts has helped us move on. Even today's events will not bring closure. He will always be gone, but we will move on. Dan's spirit and positive energy keep us going. We forgive not for him, but because of him.

"Our healing process is ongoing, but to spend the rest of our lives with bitterness, anger and hate in our hearts would end up destroying us and causing us more more pain. We forgive because Dany has shown remorse to our family, and has privately held himself accountable. We know that the remorse he has shown is genuine, sincere and from his heart. We forgive because we know Dany's intentions that night were not to cause harm to Dan. There was no forethought or intent. None whatsoever. We truly believe that.

"Where do we go from here? We feel that even though such a tragic event has happened, something positive can come from it. We want to see Dany be a healthy contributing member of society. We and others want to see him play hockey, which is what he does. We do not want his career jeopardized with any kind of jail sentence or deportation issues. As much as we would like to, we can't go back in time. Dany can't either. We can only go ahead, as we know Dan would want it. Dany has a burden to carry for the rest of his life. He plays for Dan now, too, and he always will."

243

Next it was Jake's turn. He had worked on his statement in the days before the family left Elmira for Atlanta. He'd practised it over and over to ready himself for the moment before the judge. Yet when the time came, he was too overcome with emotion, and again Graham had to resume his role, as he had so often, as his family's spokesman.

"Jake has asked that I read what he has prepared," Graham said. "Your Honour, I would like to thank you at this time for the opportunity to have both my own voice and that of my family heard in this courtroom today. My first thoughts at the time of my brother's passing were that not only had I lost my brother, but I also lost my best friend. After many brotherly arguments, battles and fights during our childhood, we became much closer in the last 10 years. I got to see first-hand a brother live out everything that we had both dreamed of as young boys. I also got to see him as he won two championships on the way to a career in the NHL, events that are etched in my memory forever.

"Unfortunately, it's moments like this I won't get to experience ever again. No more championships to be won or lengthy discussions about the sport that we both love so much. I will not have him stand beside me at my wedding, nor I at his, as we both had said that we will do some day. Nor will he get to meet my first child. If it is a son, of course, he would be named after my brother. Thinking about all of that — all that has been lost, has left me tired at times, sleepless at others, and kept me from my job recently. Twenty-five years of having Dan Snyder as a brother are 25 years I'm very happy to have had, but most of the time it feels like it wasn't near long enough.

"A lot of time has been spent over the last 16 months on

thoughts such as these, but much of what has happened in that time has also been positive. The support of not only our community but the entire hockey world has been overwhelming. In many ways, that is a testament to the closeness of our hometown and the generosity of hockey people around the world. But it is also a testament to the effect that my brother had on people's lives. This is the Dan Snyder that I want to tell you about today. I made a promise to Dan when I was in the hospital. I told him that the world would know the strength and courage he displayed right up until his death. I also said that those who didn't know who he was would hear about the wonderful person that I knew. I have never known anyone that cared about those around him more than my brother. Whether it be spending countless hours for various charitable causes, lending a sympathetic ear to those closest to him, Dan could always be counted on. And that is something that I think needs to be considered today.

"I think if time permitted, we could fill this courtroom with teammates of Dan's and hear man after man tell everyone what a great teammate he was. He also put the goals of his team in front of his own, and that is what made him a great leader, a great captain and a great friend. Dany Heatley is one of those people my brother counted on as a teammate, a friend and also a roommate. During the time the two were roommates, I never had the opportunity to meet Dany in person, but from the way my brother spoke of him, I knew he was a good friend. It is Dan's goodwill and spirit of friendship that needs to be recognized when sentencing Dany Heatley.

"Unfortunately, my brother cannot speak for himself today, but as his brother, and also for my sister, I feel it is my responsibility to do so. I spoke of two things that I would do at the time of Dan's funeral. One point that I made was if Dany Heatley was one of Dan's guys, he was one of my guys. Dany and I have become friends since that time, and in getting to know him, I know he never intended for this to happen. Secondly, I mentioned that I would try and spend the rest of my life trying to be more like my brother. To honour Dan's memory properly, I believe I need to be as helpful to Dany Heatley as not only [I would be to] a friend of mine, but a friend of my brother's. I don't want to see my friend go to prison and I know in my heart Dan would feel the same way."

With the plea Heatley had entered, he was leaving his fate in the judge's hands. In accordance with the Snyders' wishes that Heatley not have to face deportation issues, the prosecution agreed in their sentence recommendations not to ask for jail time. But the judge could have overruled both parties and given Heatley the maximum sentence. Observed from afar, Georgia might appear to be one of those monolithic "red" states — having voted 60 percent in favour of President George W. Bush in the presidential election of 2004 three months earlier. And as much as some of the neighbouring suburbs of Atlanta — like Tom Langley's Cobb County — and the state's rural areas are hardcore law-and-order jurisdictions, Fulton County is more diverse and complex. Before the Great Depression, Fulton County comprised the City of Atlanta almost exclusively, with Milton County to the north and Campbell County to the south. But during the Depression, those two counties went bankrupt and Fulton annexed them.

The present-day result makes for an odd demography and geography — the county's farthest points are some 70 miles apart. Outside the city limits to the north, the county is affluent and predominantly white, home to country clubs and where many of the Atlanta Braves live. South of the city, near the sprawling airport — one of the country's busiest — tends to have a working class flavour and is predominantly African-American, as many whites fled the area's older suburbs when the courts ordered the racial integration of schools. Farther south still, Fulton is white and rural. Much of the county's political power-base still leans towards the liberal from supporters within the city. So to think the judges who serve the county are uniformly conservative would be a mistake.

Portly and folksy, Judge Barnes could be found in his chambers wearing an oversized cowboy-style belt buckle. Balding with a gray beard, he showed a self-deprecating sense of humour at the hearing and a sensitivity to the Snyders' plight. Tragically, Barnes was gunned down in his courtroom, along with court reporter Julie Brandau, just six weeks later, when a defendant overpowered a sheriff's deputy and stole her gun. After his passing, defence attorneys spoke of the paradox that Brian Nichols killed Barnes for what he saw as a symbol of a racist system, when Barnes was the kind of man who would clear his calendar around Christmas to hold marathon sessions that helped ensure as many defendants — many of whom would have been black — as possible could be home for the holidays. The district attorney later conceded that he believed that no matter how harshly he tried to prosecute Heatley, the judge would not have sentenced him to jail. Brett Pinion, one of the assistant prosecutors, spoke of a case he had tried before Barnes that was adjudicated almost one year before Heatley's, on February 16, 2004. In that case, a convicted felon named Perry Covert was involved in a double vehicular homicide in which a child also suffered serious bodily injury. To Pinion's shock, Barnes sentenced Covert to five years of probation.

Barnes addressed the Snyders after Graham and Jake concluded their statements. "Mr. Snyder, Southerners are full of phrases. You may not know that, but, you know, we talk about folks not having a dog in the hunt, you know, they really don't have any business poking their nose into it, and so forth and so on. As you were talking, some phrases came to my mind like, 'You're a better man than I, Charlie Brown.' I don't know that I could do this if I were you, you know. I also can't help but think, and, of course, your son is not here, Jake is here, Dan is not, but my guess is that you all are — and this is not necessarily a Southern phrase — cut from the same cloth, and also that the acorn did not fall far from the tree.

"I want to thank you all, and the rest of your family who chose not to stand before this court, for coming before this court and saying the things that you did. And I know that your regard for Mr. Heatley is high and your forgiveness is great. And, in part, that's one of the reasons why the parties in this case, Mr. Heatley and the State of Georgia, have been able to come together and, in part, reach an accord. It takes a lot to do what you're doing. Thank you. Jake, thank you very much. Mr. Snyder, thank you."

The judge then asked Garland to proceed. He introduced Rutherford Seydel, who made a brief statement to the court on Heatley's behalf. Then it was Heatley's chance to address the court. His hair was at its trademark kinkiest, but gone was the self-assured attitude of a world-class athlete. His voice choked with emotion, he began.

"First and foremost, I want the court to understand that no matter what happens here today, my thoughts are about and with my friend Dan Snyder and with his family. I want to let them know that I'm sorry for what I did. I can't begin to imagine how hard Dan's death has been on them. Even with all the grief Dan's death has brought, I thank them . . ." he turned to look at them and named them, "Graham, LuAnn, Jake and Erika, for standing by me since this happened. They're truly amazing, compassionate people. And I would like to say to them right now, with all my heart, I'm truly sorry for the loss of their son and brother.

"The past 16 months have also been a very difficult time for me and my family. The support of the Snyder family has meant everything to me. The mistake I made that night was driving too fast, and this mistake will stay with me for the rest of my life. Dan Snyder was not only a great teammate and a great person, he was also a great friend. We were both young players starting our careers with the Atlanta Thrashers. We had some great times as friends and teammates. I consider myself lucky to have had a friend like that at that time.

"No matter what else happens in my life, Dan's memory will always be with me, and so will the pain with what I did. I will do everything I can to use my influence as a person and hockey player to help other young people so they do not make the same mistake that I did. I accept whatever punishment this court thinks I should receive. Thank you."

At that point, Judge Barnes asked Murray and Karin Heatley if they had anything they would like to say. Murray Heatley, in particular, was caught up with emotion and declined the offer.

"Your Honour, as you can imagine, it's a very emotional moment for them," Garland said. At the judge's suggestion, the Heatleys, along with Dany's brother Mark, moved from the gallery to stand next to Dany before the judge pronounced his sentence. "I just wanted you all to know, as with Mr. and Mrs. Snyder and the family, that, as a judge, I appreciate the fact that you are here, that you are standing beside your son in these times. I can't tell you the number of cases that we, this court, goes through in a year, where the defendants who are Mr. Heatley's age and sometimes younger are standing alone, have no one with them."

Garland then had one last opportunity to address the court. He noted that "the case has received the most intense, scientific analysis, investigative analysis and reflection by the state's prosecutors and their experts. . . . We believe and submit to the court that a sentence on the counts that we have submitted to you for a plea of guilty allows there to be a complete and full justice. We believe that when the Snyders said they do not want to see Dany Heatley go to jail or be unable to enter this country, that that is a just suggestion to the court."

After a summation, Garland yielded to the state. Assistant District Attorney Shondeana Crews handled the matter. "It is the state's position that the state always wanted Mr. Heatley to take responsibility for his actions. At this point in time, he has done that. In addition to that, the state did have the opportunity on a number of occasions to speak to the Snyder family. I personally have spoken to them at length. They've always indicated their wishes in reference to Mr. Heatley not receiving any type of jail time. It is the office policy that we do take into consideration the victim's family's wishes in reference to this case." She acknowledged that the district attorney's office found its own experts to look into whether Heatley would face deportation or would become inadmissible if he pleaded guilty to the felony charges, and that they found the same as Heatley's experts. "As a result of that, and based on the family's wishes, which is somewhat an anomaly, in that most of the times in vehicular homicides, the family normally do want us to prosecute and want the person to get jail time, this is a little bit of a different situation . . . so the state will place count one and count two on the dead docket. . . ."

Crews then went over each of the four counts that remained, asking Heatley if he still wished to plead guilty. He responded, yes to each one. Then she made her sentencing recommendations: 36 months probation, a $3,000 fine, 750 hours of public service, which would include speaking to schools about the effects of driving fast, and $25,000 in expenses for cost of the investigation. (One of the counts, driving too fast for conditions, merged with the vehicular homicide charge.) Asked for his input, Garland agreed with the recommendations, saying, "We would ask the court, in formulating the community service, to recognize that there's great potential for good to come from community service."

Then, as if he had not been asked enough times, Heatley was queried as to his pleas by the judge. He pleaded guilty again to each. The judge then announced his decision. He agreed with the probation, but put his own twist on some of the other portions. Some critics had wondered whether Heatley should retain his driver's licence. "I'm not going to pull your licence for that period of time," Judge Barnes said. He allowed Heatley to drive under the following circumstances: he could drive himself to work, to continue his education (he had taken classes at Wisconsin the previous summer), he was allowed to drive to go grocery shopping — "because you've got to eat," the judge said — he could drive for medical purposes and he could drive to fulfill his community service. The judge also ordered Heatley to take a risk-reduction class, a sort of defensive-driving class.

Barnes also addressed the type of vehicle he felt Heatley should be allowed to drive. "My initial thought with further driving restrictions is to require you to go out and buy like a 1975 Buick or Chevrolet stationwagon with a motor that's about ready to fail, okay. But I'm not going to go that far with it," he said. "However, I will prescribe — and even within this prescription, I understand that you can exceed the speed on a curvy road, and I appreciate that, but to the extent that you may feel that you want to speed again someplace, I'm going to ask you to drive a car that will have no more than six cylinders and that there be some sort of a governor or interlock device of some kind installed that will prohibit you from exceeding the speed limit of 70 miles an hour. And that's simply so you don't get run over on the freeways here in the State of Georgia and perhaps other places." He also would not allow Heatley to drive with any passengers other than a family member for his probationary period.

In regard to the community service, just with respect to the vehicular homicide charge, the judge instructed Heatley to give 50 speeches a year. And he did not limit them to high schools. "Defensive driving schools, nonprofit organizations, religious organizations, Boy Scouts, Girls Scouts, Campfire Girls, Cub Scouts; any group that would need to know about speeding," he said. "And the subject of these talks should be themes such as speed on the ice, not on the streets, or take the slow road and arrive alive, or something along those lines,"

The judge then approved the $25,000 fine and the probation on the other counts and their fines. Then he offered a rationale for the sentence: "I understand the gravity of what we're dealing with, Mr. Heatley. And I understand that any ounce of punishment that the state extracts will come nowhere near touching the punishment that you have been submitting yourself to. I understand the accidental nature of the accident itself. I've also driven on Lenox Road and I know how dangerous that road is even at the posted speed. And I think it's what, 35 miles an hour? . . . And I just know you're going to be living with this for a long time. . . .

"The reason I am assessing this sentence is because, first of all, the Snyders want it that way. Secondly, I don't think that the community will benefit by your being imprisoned, and I don't think the community will benefit by your inability to practise, at least for this period of time, your chosen occupation. In our pretrial conferences, we've discussed the issue of deportation and not allowing you to come back into the country. I don't think that will help you. I don't think it will help your parents. I don't think it will help the community. I don't think it will help the State of Georgia. And that's why I've imposed this punishment.

"I will say one more thing, Mr. Heatley, and then I'll be done. There will come a time when the thought will cross your mind that this sentence is too harsh. And it may come when you're scheduled for a speech and you want to sleep. It may come when the scheduling of probation reporting, and the payment is just inconvenient. I know it's going to come. And the only thing I would say to you is I would ask you to remember this, that your sentence is light as compared with the sentence of Dan Snyder."

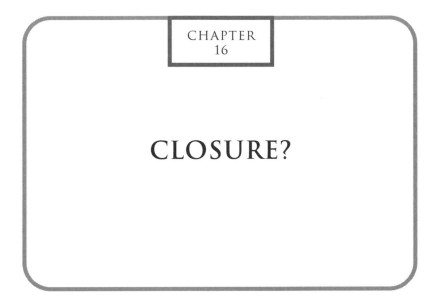

CHAPTER
16

CLOSURE?

Judge Barnes thanked the lawyers involved for their professionalism before concluding the hearing. In tears, LuAnn Snyder walked over to Dany Heatley and embraced him warmly. Friends and other members of the families did the same. The tense mood that had prevailed inside the courtroom was gradually replaced by one of exhausted relief. Outside the courthouse on Central Avenue on an unseasonably warm February day, Paul Howard, Ed Garland, Don Waddell and Graham and Jake Snyder took turns talking to the large assemblage of media as cars whizzed by. Heatley chose to speak to the media the following day from Philips Arena — a place where, ironically, he was locked out of playing at the time by the Thrashers and the NHL. In a few days, he would depart for Russia, where he would sign a contract to play with AK Bars Kazan, the same team Ilya Kovalchuk was playing with — and that Slava Kozlov would soon join. Heatley would play hockey, as the Snyders intended. "It's what he does," as Graham put it.

In the months ahead, Heatley would begin giving his talks to schools, and the Snyders could begin to go back and live their private lives, out of the public eye — though Judge Barnes' death did serve to drag them back in. Graham Snyder talked about how he had become more recognizable carrying out his daily affairs in Elmira, but joked that he'd told his business partner, "Someone needs to knock this halo off my head."

As simple as their act of forgiveness seemed to them, many still held them in anything but ordinary regard. As Dan's best friend Ryan Christie commented, "Not everybody's like that family. They don't realize it, but everybody else does."

In regard to Heatley, the restorative dimension of the Snyders' concept of justice had taken hold. There was the firm hope among many that the tragedy of Dan Snyder's death could serve some greater good by somehow preventing it from happening to someone else. When someone like Dany Heatley, a role model — whether he or others like him are aware of it — is involved in such a high-profile legal situation, the implications are far-reaching. Mark Johnson, Heatley's assistant coach at Wisconsin, spoke personally about the topic.

"My tenth-grader idolizes Dany," he said. "Like anything in life, there are lessons to be learned. . . . Kids so young make so much money and people think they can handle that. But it's not that way. People think they are mature and that they make great decisions."

In his speeches, Heatley would have to continue to deal with his mistakes in a very public forum, as he will throughout his pro hockey career, facing queries from the media as he travels from city to city. As he has said, the knowledge that he caused his friend's death will be with him forever. But as much as his contrition will be public, his own path to healing will continue to be private. The day after the hearing that kept him out of jail, he admitted to thinking of Snyder each game before he plays.

"There's certain things I do," he said. "Certain — I don't know if you want to call them superstitions or tributes — but I'll keep that just with myself," he said. Edmonton Oilers coach Craig MacTavish, when he was playing for the Boston Bruins, spent a year in jail in Massachusetts for a vehicular homicide that caused him to miss the 1984–85 season. In resuming his career in the forgiving hockey brotherhood, MacTavish became a respected player and coach. But he does not talk about that experience, in large part because he has yet to explain it to his young children. Such dilemmas are just some of the issues that Dany Heatley, too, will have to deal with some day. But as Slava Kozlov counselled him, he cannot think about it every day.

In fact, on August 9, 2005, about two weeks after the NHL lockout ended, Heatley phoned Don Waddell to ask for a trade. He wanted to make a fresh start. Heatley had sold his residence in Buckhead on December 30, 2004, and in the 16 months after the 2003–04 season, he rarely set foot in Atlanta except to defend himself in court. On August 23, 2005, Waddell was able to satisfy Heatley's wishes. In exchange for three-time All-Star right wing Marian Hossa and defenceman Greg de Vries, who won the Stanley Cup with Colorado in 2001 under Thrashers coach Bob Hartley, Waddell sent Heatley to the Ottawa Senators. Greeted to a hero's welcome at the Corel Centre when he was introduced the day after the trade, Heatley would resume his NHL career in the Canadian capital, facing more media and fan scrutiny than ever.

With her family's demands by the media sated as they departed the courthouse on February 4, 2005, LuAnn Snyder's thoughts turned to the spot on Lenox Road where events had spilled out of control more than 16 months earlier. She had never visited the site before. Graham Snyder did not think he had the will to go, but LuAnn felt compelled to see it, and Heatley's agent Stacey McAlpine chauffeured them to the site of the accident.

About eight miles north of downtown Atlanta, the buildings change from the grimy urbanity of an aging city to smart new construction enveloped by attractive landscaping and upscale shopping centres. With the remnant of Dan's watch in her pocket, LuAnn saw the rise in Lenox Road and the slight curve as it suddenly turns downhill. She thought about the aluminum car shorn in half and the speeds Heatley was alleged to have driven.

"Graham felt physically ill, but I just had to go," she said. "It felt like a closing of a chapter to me to actually see where the accident took place. When Stacey crested a small rise in the road and said, 'Here, on the left, that's where it happened,' my immediate thought was, 'There is no way he could have been going as fast as the police said he was. No way.' I got out of the car and just walked over there and stood for a bit. As I looked around, I kept thinking the same thing. I can't say I even felt emotional at the moment. I just had to see it. But that same thought kept playing over and over in my head — there's no way he could drive 80 miles per hour at this stretch of road."

In the time since her son died, and she'd felt that physical connection to him lapse with his passing, many thoughts have haunted LuAnn. What if Dan had not contracted an infection? What if he had fought it off? Would his physical or mental condition have been a cruel prison for his former athletic self — the kind of person, as LuAnn once put it, who possessed the quickness and dexterity to catch the wings off a fly? Those questions are all unanswerable.

Less than two months before the hearing, Reverend Ruth Anne Laverty, the Snyders' minister at the Elmira Mennonite Church, delivered a sermon about hope and healing. LuAnn intended to go that day, but, unknown to her, Graham had planned a surprise 30th wedding anniversary cruise to the Caribbean. Had she been present, she would have heard Laverty make reference to St. Paul's famous letter to the Corinthians — a reading used at many wedding ceremonies, its message transcends the kind of love between a husband and wife. It could just as easily describe the love felt by a mother, a father, a brother, a sister, a teammate or a friend:

Love never fails. Prophecies will cease, tongues will be silent, knowledge will pass away. Our knowledge is imperfect and our prophesying is imperfect. When the perfect comes, the imperfect will pass away. When I was a child I used to talk like a child. When I became a man I put childish ways aside.

Now we see indistinctly, as in a mirror; then we shall see face to face. My knowledge is imperfect now; then I shall know even as I am now. There are in the end three things that last: faith, hope and love, and the greatest of these is love.

DONATIONS CAN BE MADE TO:

Dan Snyder Memorial Fund
Royal Bank of Canada
6 Church St. West
Elmira Ontario, Canada N3B 1M3